THE EVERYTHING KIDS' Online Book

E-mail, pen pals,
live chats, home pages,
family trees, homework,
and much more!

Rich Mintzer
and Carol F. Mintzer

Adams Media Corporation
Holbrook, Massachusetts

An Everything® Series Book.
Everything® is a registered trademark of Adams Media Corporation.

Published by Adams Media Corporation
260 Center Street, Holbrook, MA 02343
www.adamsmedia.com

ISBN: 1-58062-394-8

Printed in the United States of America

J I H G F E D C B A

Library of Congress Cataloging-in-Publication Data available from publisher.

This publication is designed to provide accurate and authoritative information with regard to the subject matter covered. It is sold with the understanding that the publisher is not engaged in rendering legal, accounting, or other professional advice. If legal advice or other expert assistance is required, the services of a competent professional person should be sought.
- From a Declaration of Principles jointly adopted by a Committee of the American Bar Association and a Committee of Publishers and Associations

Many of the designations used by manufacturers and sellers to distinguish their products are claimed as trademarks. Where those designations appear in this book and Adams Media was aware of a trademark claim, the designations have been printed in initial capital letters.

Cover illustrations by Joseph Sherman
Interior illustrations by Michelle Dorenkamp and Kathie Kelleher
Series Editor: Cheryl E. Kimball
Puzzles by: Beth Blair

Puzzle Power Software by Centron Software Technologies, Inc. was used to create puzzle grids.

This book is available at quantity discounts for bulk purchases.
For information, call 1-800-872-5627.

Contents

CHAPTER 1 ↖ What Is the Internet?/1

CHAPTER 2 ✋ Welcome to the World of E-Mail/19

CHAPTER 3 ↖ Good and Bad Web Sites/37

CHAPTER 4 ✋ A Host of Kid-Friendly Web Sites/53

CHAPTER 5 ↖ Making Your Own Web Page/93

Fun Web Sites/107

For Parents IMPORTANT/110

A Web-Comfortable Family And Too Much of a Good Thing!/116

Acknowledgments

We'd like to thank Cheryl Kimball and Adams Media for giving us the opportunity to write this book. Also thanks to Sarah Larson and Pam and Rob Liflander. A special thank you to Dave Lipschitz for helping with computer troubles as always and to Jennifer and Stacey Lipschitz for suggesting sites.

And we'd like to dedicate the book to Rebecca Mintzer and Eric Mintzer who helped us evaluate some of the good and bad fun sites. The Internet will be a powerful tool in their future and in the future of all our children. It is already impacting heavily on the lives of all of us through e-commerce, education, business, and entertainment. It is a communications tool that is stepping to the forefront of our culture much the way television did when the baby boomer generation was young. However, this new medium is a two-way street, allowing our children to interact as no medium has ever done before. When you see your 10-year-old at the computer e-mailing or chatting with a 10-year-old in Europe or Australia, you can begin to see the wide-reaching possibility of the Internet. Just ask Jeeves! Our goal in this book is to help children familiarize themselves and become comfortable with the Internet. It is also to guide parents in facilitating their child's development with this great new medium. Happy surfing!

CHAPTER 1

What Is the Internet?

Good question!

The Internet is a large **network** of information that comes, via computer, from all over the world. It is made up of a smaller network linked together by wires and cables that send computer messages from one place to another, just like the telephone sends your voice from one place to another.

Usually, the information you see on your computer screen is in a Web site. A Web site is hard to describe. It's a place someone creates to provide information that can be seen on a computer. The information can be in the form of words, pictures, or even moving videos. The site can have all kinds of images and special effects. But what makes being on the Internet so much fun is that it is interactive. That means not only can you sit and read the message, or watch the video, you can also be involved with it. For example, by clicking on the computer **mouse,** you can turn things on and off, move to different parts of the Web site or go to another Web site. You can ask questions, answer questions, play games, and even communicate with your friends! You can't do that with television.

The Internet is like a **cyberspace** library. It brings many Web sites together so you can choose which ones you want to look at. Some sites are made up by huge companies and others are run by one or two people. Nearly every company you can think of, as well as many famous (and not so famous) people, has a Web site.

WORDS to KNOW

network: a group of computers that are linked together.

mouse: the little gadget attached to your computer with a tail-like cord that moves the arrow on your computer screen.

```
I do not fear computers,
I fear the lack of them.

-science fiction author
        Isaac Asimov
```

These sites provide information, photos, the latest news, games, film clips, and all kinds of "stuff" for you to look at on your computer. Even your friends can have a Web site . . . even you can have a Web site. In chapter 5, we'll give you some pointers on how to create one of your own.

To bring one of these millions of Web sites onto the screen of your computer, your mom or dad will first have to sign up with an **Internet service provider**, which is a company, like NetZero or America Online, that hooks you up to the Internet. Once your family is "Internet ready" (signed up), you can call up a Web site by typing in the Web address. A software program sends the Web address over your computer modem through cable lines to a central computer called a "server." The server then connects you to the site you are looking for.

It's like dialing a telephone. You punch in the numbers and your telephone connects to the phone service you are using, which then connects you to the phone number you dialed. A telephone rings on the other end and someone answers it—or not. You may not always get through when you call up a Web site either. Sometimes a site isn't working (just like when no one is home to answer the telephone). Usually, though, you'll be connected within seconds to the Web site you are looking for.

At the turn of the century an estimated 75 million Internet users were online all over the world. Some people use the Internet for work; others use it to shop. Doctors use it to look up the right medicine, writers to find the right quotes, and vacationers to plan the perfect trip. You might use the Internet to communicate or to play games or

WORDS to KNOW

cyberspace: the name for all of the online stuff going on "out there."

Internet service provider: a company that hooks you up to the Internet.

www.fastlaughs

Y did the
(:> X the

Answer: 2 get 2 the other side!

Who Knows All the Web Site Names?

A company called Network Solutions, Inc., working with the U.S. government, used to be the only entity that registered and tracked all of the millions of Web site domain names. Now there are over two dozen companies, or registrars as they are called, in the United States that can register your Web site. However, these registrars must be accredited by ICANN (Internet Corporation for Assigned Names and Numbers), a nonprofit organization that assumed responsibility from the U.S. government for registering names.

even to get help with your homework. The Internet has a lot of information on all sorts of subjects. Throughout this book, we'll give you ways to find some of that information and to enjoy games and activities.

But First, Some (Non-Boring) History

For those of you who want to know how long the Internet has been around, you may be surprised to discover it actually began over thirty years ago. The Internet started as a U.S. Defense Department project to help branches of the military (the army, navy, air force, and marines) send each other information in different parts of the country and the world. In the early 1990s, the National Science Foundation took over the Internet. They decided that people and companies would use the Internet to make money. The Internet looked as if it might be a neat place for people to communicate with each other, do research, shop, and have fun. But its image needed some work. Up until the 1990s, the information on the Internet, which started as a place for scientists to do research, was really technical and not too interesting to the general public.

The World Wide Web and HTML changed everything. But wait, isn't the Internet and the World Wide Web the same? The World Wide Web is the graphical part of the Internet, a system of Internet servers that support documents formatted in HTML (HyperText Markup Language). It's HTML that allows your Web page to link to other documents and Web sites or enables you to use graphics, audio, and video files. So all Web sites are part of the Internet, but not all Internet servers are part of the World Wide Web.

In 1993, a computer program called Mosaic came up with an easy way for anyone to use the Web. Things really took off! By the end of 1995, the World Wide Web was the place for businesses of all sorts to have sites. By the start of 2000, it seemed as if everyone had a Web site! Now you are ready to check out the Web and see what there is to enjoy.

www.hiddennumbers

Remember that little bits of information made up of zeros and ones are hiding behind everything you see on your computer screen. Circle all the zeros and ones hiding in this e-mail from Andrew to his grandmother.

Dear Grams,

Yesterday I went to a carnival at the zoo with my friends Leon and Tyrone. There was lots to do! We gazed into a mirrored maze room. (We didn't go in.) We watched one zebra and two bison eat a pile of hay with honey. (Tyrone thought the bison was phoney.) They took meat from the freezer out to the lioness. The lion even ate bacon! We played Spin The Wheel and Leon won a prize rose. (It made him sneeze.) It was so hazy and hot we wanted to buy a dozen ice cream cones from a man with a freezer on wheels. (We didn't.) Soon everyone but me was tired. They decided to doze on empty benches, but I rode on every ride. I went on the "Crazy Daze Rodeo" machine twice!

Love, Andrew

P.S. At night, every sign was neon except for one!

WORDS to KNOW

URL: stands for Uniform Resource Locator. It is the address for a Web site.

favorites: a list of your favorite Web sites that you can access easily.

Web Addresses

We told you earlier that to get to a Web site, you will need to type in a Web address. What is a Web site address?

Just as houses have addresses so you can find them, Web sites have Web addresses. The **URL** (Uniform Resource Locator) is the address of the Web site.

It usually begins with "www," which stands for the World Wide Web. First you type in the address, which is www followed by a period, and then the name of the site. Don't put in any spaces. It should look like this: *www.nameofsite*. The last part of the address will be ".com" or something similar. It tells you what type of business or organization is running the site.

When you type in a site, **be careful to notice the letters at the end**. The most common ending is ".com," which is generally for an online commercial business site (usually a company or a store). But you'll also find ".net," which is short for an online network, ".org" for organization (or an association that has a Web site), ".edu" for an educational place like a school, ".mil" for the military, or ".gov" for a branch of the government.

Type these letters in carefully or you'll get the wrong site. It's like the difference between 500 Park Avenue in Boston and 500 Park Avenue in New York. They're not even close.

A Web site address will look like *www.yahooligans.com*, which is the address for a Web site called Yahooligans.

You might also see a backslash (/) and then another word after it. That means you are being sent to a certain part of the Web site. It's like when you send a letter to an apartment building, you often need to include the apartment number. For example, the CIA (Central Intelligence Association) Web site for kids at *www.cia.gov/kids* takes you to the kids' part of the Web site. (They're cool, because they're spies!)

How-To

Favorite Places

There is usually a place on top of the screen that says **Favorites** or Favorite Places. It's like having a remote control button to take you to the Web site, or sites you love the most. If you go to a Web site that you really like, then click on Favorites or Favorite Places, it will ask you if you want to add the site to your favorite places. If you say "yes," then next time you can go right to Favorite Places and it will be there waiting for you! It's also a great thing to have in case you forgot the name of a site you really liked.

WORDS to KNOW

domain name: the name registered by the company or person that the Web site is about.

home page: the opening page that introduces the subject of the Web site.

menu: a list of options in a computer program or on a Web site.

icon: a little figure that stands for some function that is usually the same on all Web sites. For example, a little hand with the index finger sticking up means that the word or picture it is pointing to has more information buried in it. Clicking the mouse while the hand is on the word or picture will bring up the information.

The address you type in is usually the same or similar to the name of the site, or the **domain name**. Every site has a registered domain name, just like your school or library has a name. In fact, corporations often have domain names registered for each of their products.

Say you owned the Mighty Big Company, and you made hairspray, makeup, diapers, and paintbrushes (a strange combination, but hey, it's your company). You could register *www.mightybighairspray.com, www.mightybigmakeup.com, www.mightybigdiapers.com,* and *www.mightybigpaintbrushes.com* as domain names under your company and have Web sites to show your products on each of them. You might also have just one Web site called *www.mightybigcompany* and then have /hairspray or /makeup and so on. We made these up, but don't be surprised if they actually exist. It's getting harder and harder to come up with names for Web sites that aren't already out there. After all, there are millions of Web sites!

When you get to the address you're looking for, which should come up in a matter of seconds, you will usually end up on the **home page**. This is like your homeroom class in school. It's where you start, but in this case you don't even have to leave your chair. You can go to any number of places by moving the mouse and clicking the left button.

Some sites have a **menu** of choices (like in a restaurant). Many sites have **icons** (or little pictures) that stand for some function. When you move the mouse around, the little arrow will turn into a pointing finger when it lands on an icon.

Underlined words, often in blue or some other color, will also turn the arrow into a pointing finger. That means you can click right there to see something else. Even though in general it's not polite to point, on the Internet, it's okay.

Navigating

Navigating means getting around the Web site. You just point the arrow and click the mouse. That's why it's called **point and click.**

Some of you are pretty comfortable at the computer. You've used it at home or in school. For others the computer is new and navigating may take some getting used to. So if you know all this, you could skip the rest of the paragraph (of course, you won't know that you know it unless you read it). It's rather

WORDS to KNOW

navigate: moving around the Internet.

point and click: the nickname for when you point your mouse arrow and click it to make something happen.

Point and click

Navigate your way through this puzzle by making a path that alternates POINT and CLICK. You can travel up and down or side to side, but not diagonally. Be sure to avoid the ERROR messages!

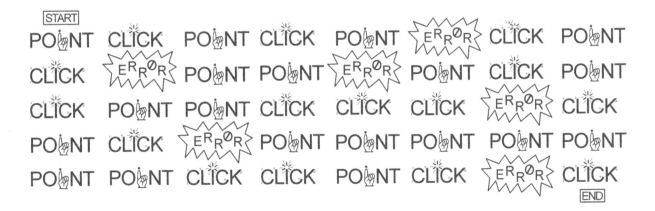

START							
POINT	CLICK	POINT	CLICK	POINT	ERROR	CLICK	POINT
CLICK	ERROR	POINT	POINT	ERROR	POINT	CLICK	POINT
CLICK	POINT	POINT	CLICK	CLICK	CLICK	ERROR	CLICK
POINT	CLICK	ERROR	POINT	POINT	POINT	POINT	POINT
POINT	POINT	CLICK	CLICK	POINT	CLICK	ERROR	CLICK
							END

WORDS to KNOW

link and **hyperlink:** they take you to other parts of the Web site.

scroll: computer text rolling along on the screen.

download: to store a computer program from a Web site or disk to your computer.

simple. When you click on a **link** (that's when the finger is pointing to take you to another part of the site), a little hourglass will appear as the new page is loaded. If you have a fast computer, the page may come up before you can blink. If you have a slower computer, or if it is a big Web site with lots of pictures, it might take a few seconds.

The links within a Web page are actually called **hyperlinks**, but that's not important. What matters is that you find what you're looking for or discover something new and cool. If you don't like what you see after clicking on the hyperlink, move the arrow to the Back button on the upper portion of the screen (usually toward the left), and click. That will send you back to the previous screen. You never have to stay on a Web page you don't like!

If you like what you see and want to go down the page and see what else there is, move the mouse so the arrow is on the up or down arrows on the right side of the page. Then, click to **scroll** up or down, which moves the page up or down on the screen.

Consider This

Everyone Is Doing It

Let's face it, there are a lot of copycats out there! Ever since one of the big search engines came out with a kids' version of its site, everyone's doing it. There is now Yahooligans from Yahoo, Lycos for Kids from Lycos, Webcrawler for Kids from Webcrawler, and plenty of others.

Downloading

Moving a program from the Internet, or from software, onto your computer is called **downloading**. The program usually goes into the computer's hard drive, where all information is saved. Many online games will ask you to download a program called Shockwave. Other games may ask for other programs. Usually the downloads are simple. The Web site has a place for you to click on and do this.

Follow That Link 🖐

Click on a link and it will take you from one web site to another. Try to follow the links in this puzzle from the word "recipe" to the word "hamburger." Use the last letter of each word as the first letter of the next word. Words can go left and right, up and down, backwards, but NOT diagonally. Words can also turn a corner in the middle, or cross over words you have already found. Read all the leftover letters to spell out a basic fact about the internet. HELP: The words you are following are all food words. They are listed below - but not in order!

WORD LIST:
apples
eggs
hamburger
ice cream
mango
olives
peanut
recipe
sandwich
soup
spaghetti
strawberry
tacos
tuna
yogurt

```
START→ R E C I P E L I V
       I I W D T G O I E
       S C A N L G G L S
       E H G A P S N C T
       T A O S O C A T R
       T M B U R G M U A
       I C E C R E A N W
       P A N U T R E N B
       P L E S O U P N E
       E C T E D G O Y R R
```

WORDS to KNOW

file: where you store information on a computer.

reboot: to start your computer again.

surfing: looking around on the Internet.

search engine: a service that allows you to look things up on the Internet.

Depending on your computer, some downloads will take longer than others. Usually the site will tell you how long it will take. It could be anywhere from a few seconds to several minutes. Sometimes the game you want to download will require that you have some other program already on your computer. You may need to ask your mom and dad if you have that program. In fact, you should always ask your parents if it's okay to download programs.

Sometimes you will be asked if you want to save the download into a permanent or temporary **file**. If you want to play the games again, you can hit "permanent" so the program will stay in your computer on your hard drive. Sometimes you have to "restart" the computer. That means you have to get off the computer and then go back on, a process called **rebooting**.

Once again, ask your parents to show you how or to help you until you are used to shutting down and restarting the computer.

You may also need to download different versions of Shockwave or other programs separately. For example, the Shockwave program you have from previous games may not work with the game you want to play now, or you may need another part, like Shockwave "Flash." Just follow the download instructions and it should work.

Web Searching (Surfing the Web)

You'll probably hear a lot of talk about **surfing** the Internet these days. Many TV commercials advertise popular Internet sites. Companies like Yahoo!, Excite, America Online, Info Seek, and Lycos are popular service providers that put you onto the Internet and let you search the World Wide Web. Once you

How-To

Say What You Mean

When you search the Web, try to be really clear about what you are looking for. If you want information on George Washington, don't just type in Washington. You will get information on the state of Washington or on Washington, D.C. In fact, even if you type in George Washington, you may still get information on the George Washington Bridge or George Washington High School. Type in George Washington President and that should help narrow the search.

Consider This

Too Many!

When you search for something, (on a site that isn't just for kids), you should ask for help until you (and your mom or dad) feel that you are ready to do it alone. You may get a huge number of "results" or Web sites. Sometimes you'll see a number like 854,000! Don't panic—the first five to 10 sites on the list are usually the closest matches. If they don't turn up what you want, type in your search again, using different words

are signed up, that site will be your link to the Internet. Most of these service providers have a lot of their own channels like sports, entertainment, and news headlines. They also have a place where you can search for a Web site.

The **search engine** part of the Web site will help look up information. In fact, no matter which provider you have, you can use any search engine. Type in the name of the search engine where you type in the Web site address.

You can try www.yahoo.com, www.go.com, www.lycos.com, www.aol.com, or www.excite.com. Each search engine is like a superfast librarian who will search the Web and find you a whole bunch of Web sites on your subject. They can find hundreds or thousands of Web sites, which is why you should have a grown-up help you. Better yet, use these search engines made for kids:

- Route 6–16 at www.cyberpatrol.com/616
- KIDS CLICK at http://sunsite.berkeley.edu/kidsclick!/
- Supersnooper at www.supersnooper.com
- Education World at www.education-world.com

These search engines are more fun because you will find what you are looking for much quicker. Also, after a short time of getting used to the search engine, Mom and Dad might let you look on your own.

How Do Search Engines Work?

All search engines work in pretty much the same way. You will find a blank rectangle with the word "search" beside it. The box is the place where you can type in whatever it is you want to find.

Here's an example: Let's say you are looking for magic tricks for kids. Type in "magic tricks for kids" and wait for a list of sites with brief descriptions. You will be able to go down the page and choose the ones you want to look at. Since there are

www.correctaddress

Want to make sure your e-mail doesn't get lost? Want to get to the right web site without taking a wrong turn? Then you must make sure each letter of the address is correct. Find the one and only time that the word "address" is spelled correctly in the letter grid. Search carefully - it could be up, down, left to right, backwards, or even diagonally!

```
RADEDDAADADDRE
ADRESSDRADDRES
DDEASADDRESAAA
ARSADDDRESSDED
AESDDRERDSEDSD
DADREDESSEARRE
RSSESRRSSADSDS
EADDRESESADRES
ADRESESASDREDD
DRESSADRESESAD
```

many Web sites and the computer looks for them by each word you type in, you may also get sites that are on other subjects. The cool thing about the kids' search engines is that they are set up to look for the best ones for you! You will get maybe 10 awesome Web sites about magic, not hundreds and hundreds like on the bigger search engines.

Sometimes when you search for something, if you put words together with an "and" sign (&) or a "plus" sign (+), the search engine will only look for sites that have those words together. This way you won't get so many sites. You might look for Barbie+Doll+Houses, or Barbie&Doll&Houses instead of Barbie Doll Houses. It depends on the search engine. As you search with your parents, you will figure out the best way to search on different engines.

Most search engines also offer a variety of subjects that you can click through to find the topic or Web page you're looking for. For example, on Yahoo you could click on Recreation>Toys>Dolls>Barbie to find a list of Barbie Web sites.

E-mail Club

Create your own online club with your friends. Make a list of names so you know who everyone is and can build an e-mail list just for the club. Set up some rules such as:

No one says anything nasty about other club members

No one gives out personal information about themselves or each other.

Pick screen names and decide which chat area you'll meet in and when. Perhaps you'll pick a topic for the evening, or the club will have a regular schedule . . . . Mondays: Pop Stars, Tuesdays: Movies, etc.

How-To

Online Agreement

Do you want to show Mom and Dad that you are responsible? Do you want to assure them that you can go online and they will not have to worry?

If you do, you might want to draw up an Internet/online agreement or a contract of sorts letting them know what you will and will not do online. In return, you might gain greater Internet independence.

For example, you might include some of the following ideas:

I agree that when I am in an Internet chat room, I will never give out any personal information about myself or my family or friends.

I will use proper online language.

I will not spend more than one hour online per day.

In return I ask that:

I will not be interrupted when I'm online.

I can go on the Internet by myself.

I can spend an extra hour online on the weekend.

Once you've listed your basic agreement, which includes what you will do and what you want, then your parents will list what they want from the agreement. Then you sit down with them and do what is called negotiating, where you say okay to some of what they want and they say okay to some of the things you want. This is also a way of compromising and making up an agreement that's good for everyone involved. Don't forget to include what happens if anyone breaks the agreement.

Once you and your parents have agreed, you will all sign the agreement and post it, perhaps on the refrigerator or near the computer.

CHAPTER 2

Welcome to the World of E-Mail

WORDS to KNOW

e-mail: letters you send and receive online.

FUN FACT

Wow!

It is very likely that at the rate e-mail is growing as a way of sending information, by the year 2002 there will be over 140 million people using e-mail in the United States (more than half of the people in the country).

E-mail, or electronic mail, is a great way to communicate with friends and relatives anywhere in the world. In fact, many people prefer e-mail to the telephone (although it is still nice to actually talk to people).

When the Internet was first created, one of its most important features was as a way to communicate. The first Internet users were the military and scientists. They wanted to be able to send each other messages quickly, messages that could not be intercepted by anyone else. Today, electronic mail is one of the most common ways for people all over the world to communicate with each other. But how does it work?

The e-mail message that you send goes to a mail server, which is usually part of your Internet provider. There are also separate e-mail systems like Juno that are designed just for sending and receiving e-mail. You don't need to have a separate system if yours is part of your service provider like AT&T or AOL. Once the server gets your message, it hooks up with the server listed on the e-mail address. Next to the screen name of the person or company that you are mailing to is the "domain name." The domain name is like the address and zip code part of an old-fashioned letter.

It directs the e-mail to the server used by that person or company. It's like the letter is going to the central post office in the recipient's city, state, or country. That server then posts it in the inbox of the person's online mailbox, which is sort of like a postal carrier delivering it.

John Smith @ aol.com

Interesting! ⬉

How many of these words do you know that start with the letters I-N-T-E-R? When you are finished, collect the letters in the shaded boxes from top to bottom. Use them to finish the word in the following sentence:

The internet is INTER▮▮▮▮▮▮. It allows two-way communication!

1. The class after "beginning",
   but before "advanced"' .... INTER_ _ _ _ ▮ _

2. A radio system that lets
   people talk between different
   rooms in a house .... INTER▮_ _ _

3. To break into a conversation
   and change the subject.......................... INTER_ _ _ _ ▮

4. A rest period between the first
   and second half of a concert. .... INTER_ _ _ ▮ _ _

5. A meeting where one
   person asks the other person
   questions about themself .... INTER▮_ _ _

6. To stop something on its way
   from one place to another....................... INTER_ ▮_ _ _

Of course, unlike sending regular mail, all of this activity takes a matter of minutes. (That's why you'll hear regular mail referred to as "snail mail.") So, if you call your friend just five minutes after sending an e-mail, chances are he or she has already received it.

One question that is often asked is whether or not you have to have your computer turned on or be online to receive e-mail. To send it, you have to go online. But to receive e-mail, you don't even have to have the computer turned on. You can be at school or at a friend's house and receive e-mail as long as your Internet server is connected.

Faster than the Postal Carrier

Perhaps the coolest thing about e-mail is that the person you are sending it to will usually receive your e-mail message within a matter of minutes (or at least the next time they sign on to e-mail). That is much faster than sending a letter through the post office.

Sending E-Mail

One of the best things about electronic mail is that it doesn't cost any more money to e-mail a friend in France than it does to e-mail your grandmother down the street. There are millions of e-mail messages sent everyday. They range from notes sent between friends to important business information sent between companies. All sorts of information is sent by e-mail. Writers send stories and even whole books (such as this one) to their editors and publishers by e-mail. Lawyers and businesspeople send contracts. People send greeting cards, look for jobs, exchange recipes, send jokes, and even forward photos of their last vacation or of their grandchildren. Except for packages, almost any message or information that can be sent by regular mail can be sent by e-mail.

Now that we've rambled on about e-mail, you're probably anxious to use it. But you will need some information first. Just like sending regular mail, you will need the address of the person to whom you are sending the message. Ask your friends and family to write down their e-mail addresses. Copy the address carefully so it will get to the right person. There is usually an @ symbol (which means "at") that tells you which e-mail provider the person is using, such as AOL or AT&T or HOTMAIL. You can e-mail us and tell us how much you like the book at *rsmz@worldnet.att.net*.

Once you type in the address, you will usually need to type in the subject. That may be anything from "Just saying hi" to "Party this Saturday at my house!" Then you are ready to type in your e-mail message. Use appropriate

Everything Kids'

http://www.

Make an Offline/Online Activity Book

Many sites have games, puzzles, and drawing activities that you can print out. To make an activity book, get a notebook or loose-leaf binder in which you can either tape, paste, or include with holes (have Mom or Dad use the hole puncher) these printouts. The book can be your very own online source of offline fun when you travel or are not on the computer.

E-Mail Tips

1. Keep it short.
2. Try not to repeat yourself.
3. Don't overuse e-mail (don't send people messages again and again and again).
4. Watch your language; don't be rude or nasty.
5. Try not to repeat yourself—just wanted to see if you were paying attention!

E-mail is super fast—it can go across the street or across the country in just a few minutes! Can you guess the new nickname for letters that are delivered by the post office? To find out, start with the letter T marked by a black dot. Travel into the center of the spiral, collecting all the letters in the dark sections. When you get to the center, start back out again. This time, collect all the letters in the white sections. Write the letters on the lines provided. Finally, connect the dots to complete a secret picture.

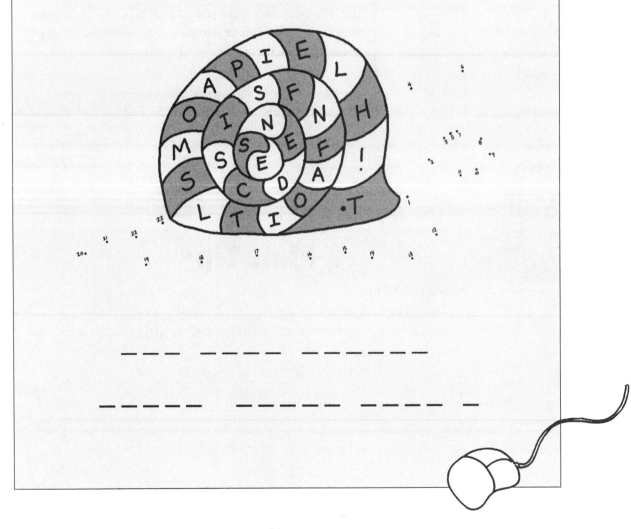

___ ____ _____

_____ _____ ____ _

language and take your time. Try not to go on too long. Be sure to look it over before you send it. You can make changes, if you need to. Then follow the directions to send it. Usually there's a Send button, but you may need to do more. Sometimes there is a Send/Receive button, as on Microsoft Outlook. Have your mom or dad help you get started with e-mail on your service provider. You can send messages to a few people at once. Right below the "To" space, you'll find a "cc" space. ("cc" stands for carbon copy—an old phrase from the days of typewriters). That's where you can type in the address of whoever else you want to receive the same message. You can use commas and put several names. Make sure you spell each one correctly, and don't forget the "at" sign (@) and the name of the server for each address. If you spell any one of the names wrong, the whole message may not go out! Type slowly.

You can also reply to someone else's e-mail by hitting Reply, and it will set up a new message for you to send out. That's easy. If the original message was sent to you and a bunch of other people, you can hit Reply to All. Or you can choose to reply to just the person who sent it by hitting Reply and it will go to the one person. Choose between these two carefully. You would be surprised how many messages people have tried to send to one friend, not realizing they'd sent it to 10 people—some of whom they didn't even know!

Receiving E-Mail

AOL coined the popular, yet sometimes annoying, phrase "You've got mail." Other service providers will let you know in other ways that you have received mail. Even if they don't send up a red flag, you can click on mail, then hit Send/Receive and your new messages will appear in your **inbox**. Just like a person

WORDS to KNOW

virus: a program designed to mess up computers. Other programs, called anti-virus software, have been created to recognize and destroy viruses.

may have an inbox on the desk at the office for letters, you will have an inbox to collect your e-mail.

Then you can click on messages to open them just as you would open mail by ripping open the envelope. It's important to see who sent you the e-mail. Sometimes it is listed by name and other times by e-mail address. *If you don't recognize the name or the address, don't open the e-mail.* It may just be an advertisement, but it could have a computer **virus** in it that will mess up the computer badly unless the computer has an anti-virus program on it. Tell Mom or Dad that they should install an anti-virus program on their computer; we'll wait.

If you open an e-mail with a computer virus, be assured that once your parents or the owner of the computer gets it fixed, it will be a long time before you get to use it again. Also, don't open e-mails addressed to

SHOUTING!!

For some reason, typing in all caps is considered SHOUTING AND IS PERCEIVED AS BEING RUDE. SINCE YOU DON'T LIKE PEOPLE SHOUTING AT YOU, DON'T TYPE IN ALL CAPS, okay?

someone else, even if they are family members.

After you have read your e-mail messages you can save or delete them. It all depends on whether you ever want to read them again. If it's a message you really liked, you may want to save it. If it's just a simple "hi, how are you doing" you may just reply and delete it. If you want to forward a message on to another friend, you can hit the Forward button and type in the friend's address and send it on. Try not to save all your e-mail, it can slow down the computer or make it difficult to download other things. It's like having too much stuff in your bedroom. You can't find a place to put new things and it slows you down trying to get through the mess.

Chatting

Chatting is the Internet way of carrying on a conversation, except instead of talking you're typing. Yes, there are computer systems where people can talk to each other, and even see each other, but they are not yet common for home use.

Chat rooms are designed as online places where several people can talk to each other at once. Obviously, they are not really rooms. They're channels where a certain number of people can all communicate with each other at one time. The channel can include people from all over the country or all over the world. All they have to do is be on the same site or server, depending on who is hosting (or who set up) the chat channel. It's like one big conference call. Since these channels can only hold a certain number of people (usually between 20

WORDS to KNOW

chat room: online places where a group of people can chat with each other in "real time" (that is, you are all on your computers at the same time). Usually chat rooms are set up to talk about a particular hobby or interest.

Keyboard Code

What information should you NEVER give out over the Internet? Find out by using the keyboard to decode the following list. HELP: The circle with a slash mark through it is the number zero, not the letter O.

Answers: Find each letter, number and punctuation mark of the secret message on the keyboard. Now for each one, locate the key in the next row down and slightly to the left. When you do this, you will find the following list of information you should NEVER give out over the Internet:

name   address   school   phone number   password   photo

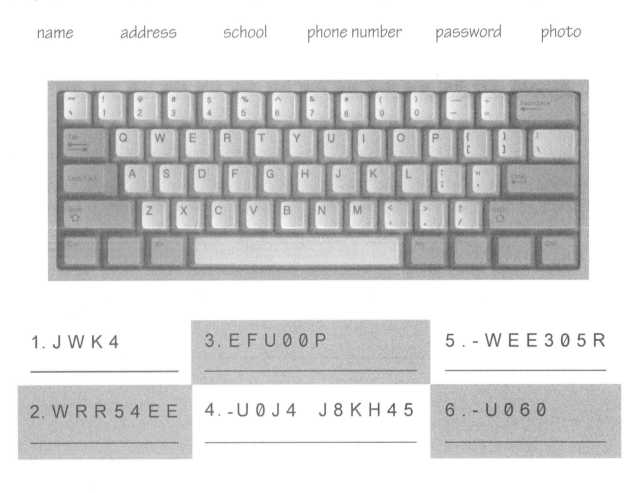

1. J W K 4
_____

2. W R R 5 4 E E
_____

3. E F U 0 0 P
_____

4. - U 0 J 4   J 8 K H 4 5
_____

5. - W E E 3 0 5 R
_____

6. - U 0 6 0
_____

and 30) at one time, you may not always be able to get into the chat room you want.

Many Web sites and Web servers set up chat rooms. And many chat rooms have specific subjects or themes. For instance, you may find a room where everyone is talking about movies or about music or science. Some rooms are just general chat rooms for talking about whatever you and the other people in the room want to discuss. You can sit back and read what other people have to say, or jump in and express yourself. You will find yourself typing messages back and forth with strangers who may become friends. Don't worry if you type slowly at first; the more you do it, the faster you'll get. Besides, in a chat room it's important to be concise and only say a little at a time.

Chat rooms for kids are available from most major servers and on many sites designed for kids. They are almost always monitored (meaning an adult is keeping tabs on what's going on, so no one says anything nasty), and they can be great fun whether you join in or sit back and read what's being said.

So that no one knows who you really are, you will have a **screen name**, which is a made-up name to use in the room—almost like a secret identity. Choose a name that you will remember and write it down someplace—then remember where you wrote it down! Also, don't be upset if the name you choose isn't available. That means someone already has that screen name and you'll have to choose a different one. There are many people talking on the Internet, so a lot of screen names are already taken. It's okay, you can have fun creating a new one! Be creative, and remember to keep your identity anonymous.

WORDS to KNOW

screen name: the fake name you create to remain anonymous when you chat online.

Consider This

Age-Appropriate Level for Chat Rooms

Chat rooms are generally not for kids under 10 or 11 years old. It's up to you and your parents. All kids' and teen chat rooms should be monitored so that no one can spoil the fun. This can even be helpful in adult chat rooms where one "bad apple" can ruin it for everyone.

WORDS to KNOW

typos: mistakes made in typing. These can be common in e-mail since you are usually writing quickly and it is considered informal. There are spell-check programs that will help you minimize typos, but they are considered no big deal in e-mail.

Before chatting, it's important to remember a few things:

1. Never give out your last name to anyone online.
2. Never give out your password to anyone online.
3. Never tell anyone where you live or give out your phone number online.
4. Don't give anyone enough information, even by accident, so they can find you. For example, don't mention a popular landmark that may be near your home.
5. Never plan to meet someone you've met on the Internet in person unless you have been talking with them for a while and your parents set up, and accompany you to, the meeting. Even when grownups meet someone online, they like to have a friend go with them—and they meet in a public place. Rarely will you want to meet an online friend, but if the topic comes up make sure your parents are involved in any planned meeting. *This is very important.*
6. If you think someone is not being honest about his or her identity, stop chatting with that person.
7. Never send anyone a photo of yourself online.
    Reread this list—it's very important!

Consider This

Errors

Don't worry too much about typos (errors or mistakes) when you are typing online. Everyone makes them because often you are typing real fast! And you are not being graded.

Etiquette

When you are in a chat room, remember to let everyone have a chance to talk. Sometimes the conversation will be among a few people and sometimes among everyone in the room. If you can't find a place to jump in, just sit back and read for a while. You can always find a chance to say "hi" when you're ready. If you are new to chat rooms, you may be shy at first—that's okay too.

How-To

Reply Again and Again

Even though you hit Reply and sent a message back to a friend on Monday, it doesn't erase the original message unless you choose to delete it. If the original message remains in your inbox, you can hit Reply and send them another message on Tuesday. Often people go back to an old e-mail and use it to reply to someone rather than typing in that person's address all over again. Many e-mail programs have address books that will store the names of people you send e-mails to frequently.

WORDS to KNOW

newbie: someone new to the chat room.

FAQ: short for frequently asked questions. You will often see a FAQ list or link in programs or Web sites.

Also, once you get comfortable and find yourself talking a lot in a chat room, remember to be polite to the new people (called **newbies**) who join the room. They may be shy at first just as you were. Don't forget you were once new at this too!

Online Language

No, don't worry, you do not have to learn a new computer language to communicate online. But there are some shortcuts that you may see. Sometimes people like to abbreviate 2 communicate what they R trying to say.

A few common online abbreviations are:

ASAP—as soon as possible (this is also common
    offline too)
BBL—be back later
BRB—be right back
BTW—by the way
DC—don't care
FAQ—frequently asked questions
FYI—for your information
    (you'll also see and
    hear this
    one offline)
GG—gotta go
LMA—leave me alone
LOL—very popular way of
    saying "laughing online" or
    "laughing out loud"
NC—no comment
THX—thanks
TTT—tell the truth
W—with

FYI BRB ASAP THX

Most people don't take too many shortcuts online, but you will see some as you chat. If you don't understand one, ask what it means. If you do cut corners, don't overdo it. B4 U use 2 many shortcuts, B sure every-1 will B able 2 understand U.

Common Internet Problems

The Internet and the Web are part of the growing technology that is an exciting part of our world. Computers and cables are the tools that make all this communication and online excitement possible. Like any other machines, however, computers and Internet servers and providers can have their problems. There are times when the server, or the main computer system that has you hooked up to the Internet, is down. This doesn't mean it's depressed; it's simply not working. A Web site also may not be working and you will get a message saying that you cannot connect with that site. Sometimes the people running the site have shut it down to make changes or work on the site. Or there may be something wrong in the connection to the Web site. Most of the time, if you can't connect with a Web site, it has nothing to do with your computer.

You may have typed in the wrong Web address, such as *www.usgoc* instead of *www.usg*. It's always a good idea to try typing in the address again if it didn't connect. The same is true if an e-mail is

Consider This

More than One Mailbox

Netscape Messenger, Outlook Express, and Juno are three examples of the many e-mail programs that you may be using. You can have more than one e-mail address, sometimes on the same program. People do this if they want to keep personal and "business" e-mail separate. You might be president of a club at school or involved in a group outside of school and want the people in that group or club to e-mail you at one address and your friends to send you e-mail somewhere else. On the Internet it can be done . . . you can have more than one mailbox.

The delete key is a very useful computer tool for getting rid of unwanted words. Use a marker or pencil to delete (cross out) any words in this e-mail that don't make sense.

Deer Hello Marta,

I can't just wait to see around you at camp the next week bend. Won't remember to bring up pictures of your same new baby sitter brother.

Your best curl friend,

Teresa :-)

returned. However, a returned e-mail can also mean that the person has changed his or her e-mail address.

Other common problems may be not being able to get online or being bumped offline. If you can't gain access to your server, it is usually because there are too many people using the same server and the lines are over-crowded. Try again later. Many service providers give a list of other phone numbers in your area that your modem can dial. There is usually a box that says Change Phone Number. Ask Mom or Dad if it is okay if you switch to another number, before changing the phone number that your computer (actually, the modem) is using to reach the service provider.

The other problem, getting booted off while you are right in the middle of looking something up or chatting with your pals, is the result of a problem on the service provider's computer or on the connection. Sometimes the connection gets interrupted momentarily. Usually, you can just go right back online. If you have "call waiting" on the telephone line that you are using to connect to the Internet, for example, and a call comes in, that can knock you offline. Ask Mom or Dad about turning off "call waiting" while you are on the computer. It's usually a matter of hitting a few buttons on the telephone. If they are not sure how to do it, remind them (nicely) that they can contact the phone company to find out.

www.fastlaughs

What does a computer do when it gets hungry?

Answer: It goes out for a byte to eat!

You can never learn less, you can only learn more.

-author
R. Buckminster Fuller

CHAPTER 3

Good and Bad Web Sites

WORDS to KNOW

banner ad: advertisements for products and services in a bar near the top of a Web site or list of sites. Banner ads are usually in color and sometimes flash to catch your attention.

What's the difference between a good and a bad Web site? What makes one site more fun or more interesting than another? Glad you asked!

Web sites emerged in the early to mid 1990s as a way of presenting information in many different ways and for a variety of reasons. Some Web sites were created to sell products (like a catalog). Some were made to give you lots of information on a subject (like a book on the topic). Some were designed for fun and entertainment (like your favorite games and TV shows). Some were made to give you a lot of information on a lot of different subjects (like an encyclopedia). Others were made by groups or organizations to let you know what they are up to (like a newsletter). Just as some movies have great special effects and others have beautiful scenery, Web sites can also have very different characteristics.

To make money, Web sites sell advertising. Some have a lot of ads flashing and others have just a **banner ad** across the top of the screen. Then the content or information is presented. When

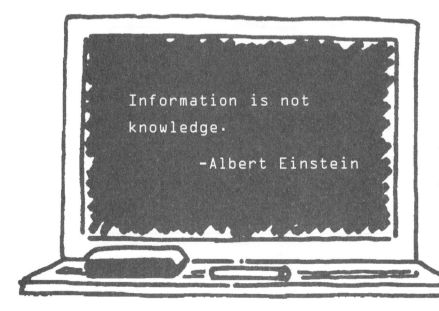

Information is not knowledge.

-Albert Einstein

Web sites were first created, many just provided basic information. Now, there are Web sites with moving images including animation, or movie and video clips. There are plenty of moving images in the games you can play online. Computer graphics are also used to make Web sites more interesting to look at. These graphics include photographs, drawings, or diagrams to highlight and show you information.

The World at Your Fingertips

No matter where you go on the World Wide Web, you need to start at your keyboard! Follow the correct path from START to the information you need. Be sure to visit the six Web sites that the search engine found for you.

Consider This

The biggest difference between a Web site and a book or television show is that a Web site is what is called **interactive**. Interactive means that you, as a visitor, are able to make things happen or not happen. You have choices. Other than choosing the channel, you cannot make a TV program any different than it already is. A book is the same whenever you read it. But a Web site lets you click your mouse to look up information, start or stop a game, play music, watch a video clip, contact an expert, or do any number of things. Therefore, a cool Web site can look good, have lots of information, lots of activities, and be interactive—letting you call the shots.

Most people find that good Web sites are **user friendly**. That means you can easily find what you are looking for and understand the directions. There are so many Web sites out there that you don't want to waste your time on ones that are hard to navigate (find your way around), confusing, or boring. As you go to more and more sites, you will discover which ones you prefer.

Unless you are looking to buy something, a good Web site shouldn't be trying to sell you everything in sight. It may have ads, but they should be clearly marked or in boxes. Sites with too

WORDS to KNOW

interactive: you can make things happen or not happen. You don't just sit and watch the screen (like TV).

user friendly: it's easy to find what you are looking for and to understand directions.

How to Recognize Good and Bad Web Sites

Good "fun" sites:

1. Give you several choices of things to do that are easy to point to, click on, and find
2. Let you get right to the game or activity with one or two clicks
3. Have clear instructions so you know how to play the game, do the puzzle, or join the chat room
4. Give you automatic downloads for games
5. Are frequently updated with new things to do
6. Don't make you wait forever for things to appear on screen
7. Are colorful and fun to look at

Bad "fun" sites:

1. Are boring because there's not enough to do
2. Make you click again and again from one place to another before you ever find anything
3. Don't tell you anything or have confusing instructions
4. Make you go someplace else for downloads
5. Take so long to get to the next screen that you get bored and give up or fall asleep
6. Stay the same month after month
7. Are either dull looking or have so much crammed on the screen that you get a headache trying to look at it all

How-To

Fan Sites

The Backstreet Boys, Britney Spears, and other popular favorites have **fan sites**. These sites range from "official" sites with pictures and fun stuff about your favs to sites created by fans like you. Some of the sites are cool and others are weird or trying to sell you stuff. It's a good idea to have someone search these sites with you to help you find the better ones, and then you can add the good ones to your favorites list.

Many people choose a screen name that tells a little something about them, like a favorite hobby. Match each "profile" (brief description of a person) to one of the screen names in the list. Write your answers in the boxes provided.

Profile List:
takes photos
has pet frog
likes comic books
lives in apartment
plays basketball
runs races
likes clocks
artistic
has pet snake
makes own lunch
goes online a lot

screen name:	profile:
laffalot	
cr8tv	
shutterbug	
surfkid	
123go	
pbj	
ribbit	
ticktock	
topfloor	
hissssss	
dribbler	

WORDS to KNOW

fan sites: Web sites about celebrities created for their fans.

many things going on at once can be confusing, because you don't know where to look first. There are also Web sites that say "coming in the fall of 1999" when it's already getting close to 2001. If the people who run the site can't keep it up-to-date, then why should you bother going there? There are good and bad Web sites.

Informational Web Sites

These are the Web sites you will go to when you are looking for homework help or simply need to find some information on a subject.

The best Web sites are the ones that help you find what you are looking for. Whether you want to play games or do homework, the good site is the one that meets your needs.

Online Shopping

www.fastlaughs

What happens when a dirty computer dies?

Answer: It bytes the dust!

Most online shopping is reserved for adults since they are the ones with the credit cards and money. However, if Mom or Dad says it's okay, then you can certainly browse some of the sites that are selling stuff. Major companies and stores, like Kids R Us, FAO Schwarz, or the Gap all have Web sites. You will also find places to shop on the Web that have no store that you could actually visit. Amazon.com is the most popular place

How to Recognize Good and Bad Information Web Sites

Good information sites:

1. Let you look up what you want without much trouble. They have a clear menu and a place to search for information.
2. Provide easy-to-understand information. They are interesting to read and have good pictures
3. Are up-to-date
4. Are backed by people who know what they're talking about (For example, many companies that publish encyclopedias and other reference books have reliable Web sites.)

Bad information sites:

1. Make you go through too many steps to get what you need
2. Are not clear in how they present information, or have so much stuff you don't know what to look at first
3. Are not up-to-date
4. Are put together by people who really don't know the answers

Good Site, Bad Site

In the following list, cross out words that:

Start with or include "UN" or "OUT"
Have the letter "W"
End in "ING"

Circle the remaining words, and you will have a description of a good Web site!

confusing	good info
quick click	unfriendly
user friendly	crowded
slow	easy-to-use
unclear	lots of choices
colorful	fast
reliable source	boring
outdated	up-to-date
unreliable	unknown

How-To

Shopping Tips

The best way to shop online is to have an idea of what you are buying from the real world. If your friend has a book that you know you want to read, or if you just heard the new Foo Fighters or TLC CD and liked it, or you just played a great new Nintendo game and want it, you'll know what you are getting when you order it. Books, games, CDs, videotapes—that stuff is easy. It gets tougher when you try buying clothes online, since you can't feel them or try them on. You need to know exactly what size you are and know what material you like to wear before ordering clothes online. Even then it's a bit risky. Things that need that "personal feel" or "personal experience" are often better purchased in a good-old-fashioned store.

A "smiley" is a little picture that you can type into your computer using punctuation marks, numbers, and letters. Can you match each smiley to the correct person or animal? HELP: Tilt your head to the left to correctly see the smilies. Here's the basic smiling face : -)

B-)	person winking
8:-)	girl with hairbow
:-)>	man with bowtie
8)	Uncle Sam
:8)	kid with braces
=I:-)	pig
:-#	man with beard
>:-)	frog
:-)8	person with glasses
;-)	alien

to buy books on the Internet, yet they do not have any actual stores that you can walk into. Sometimes it's a cool way to find stuff before the holiday season or when your birthday is coming up, so that you can make up your wish list, sort of window-shopping online.

Millions and millions of dollars are now spent each day as people buy everything from groceries to new cars online. There are even a few sites that let kids have some buying power. If you show that you can be responsible on the Internet, perhaps your parents might sign you up with Rocketcash or ICanBuy, sites that let kids do real shopping. These sites allow parents to set up an account with a certain amount of money you can spend each month, which could be something like $30. These companies are linked to several stores where you can then shop. The amount spent is put on an account and parents can cancel any orders they don't agree with. You can also save up the money and buy one bigger item after a few months, again with Mom or Dad saying it is okay. If your parents agree to let you shop online, you will see that it is important to be selective and not just buy the first thing that pops up. If your parents don't want you to shop online, that's okay too. Sometimes buying power is overrated, which means it sounds better than it really is. You should see how many people have ordered what they thought was something really cool only to find out that it wasn't all that they had expected. Don't worry, you'll be shopping in the real world soon enough.

Consider This

Double-Check

When doing your homework or looking up any information, it is always a good idea to double-check the information on more than one Web site. This can be true with any information. When the St. Louis Rams won the Super Bowl in January 2000, one Web site noted that they had won only three games in the previous season. Another Web site said the Rams had won only four games. Yet another Web site stated the Rams were victorious in only five games the previous season. Okay, so they weren't very good, but how many games did they win? Two out of the three Web sites had the wrong information.

WORDS to KNOW

secure site: a site that has a special program that allows you to send information or buy things without anyone else being able to see it.

If, and when you do get the opportunity to shop online, alone or with your parents, here are a few things to remember. (This is some stuff your parents should know too.)

1. Shop at places that are well known. Everyone knows Amazon.com or TheGap.com. These are major companies with reliable Web sites. A small unknown site may be selling things at great prices one day and be gone the next. If you're not familiar with the seller, it doesn't mean they are bad guys. You should just try to find out more about the company before sending them your money.

2. Make sure they have **secure sites**, meaning your credit card information is protected from anyone else getting the information. If the site does not specify that it is secured, ask. Most sites have a place where you can contact the company!

Shopping Web Site Treasure Hunt

While Mom or Dad is picking up groceries, you can try to find Web sites on labels and packaging. See if you can find ten for different types of products. Many companies have product information on the labels including the company Web site.

Take a small note pad along and write them down. Then when you go home you can see what they look like.

You can also take a magazine and hand one to your friend (just a regular magazine, not a computer or Web magazine) and see who finds more Web sites listed in the magazine. Articles, product and show reviews, advertisements, they all have Web sites . . . you can see who wins by finding the most.

3. Make sure the price is clearly marked. If there is any charge for shipping (sending you your stuff), it should be listed too. Any tax that is paid to the government should also be listed. They should add it all up for you and give you the total amount. You can then double-check the addition on your own calculator!

4. Print out a copy of the transaction, which means what you bought and how much you paid.

5. Look for a telephone number for the company. If they have a phone number for customer service, write it down. If something is wrong with what you ordered, you may have to call them and tell them. If they don't have a phone number, they may not be a good place to buy stuff from.

Consider This

I Can't Win!

Online games are designed at different levels. Some games are very easy while others are hard. Playing games is usually much more fun when you choose games that you find "challenging," which means you may win, but it won't be easy. Don't get upset if you don't do well at a game for a while; just keep on trying or come back and try again. If you can't understand how to play the game, then it might be for older kids. That's okay too . . . you'll be back when you are a little older!

CHAPTER 4

A Host of Kid-Friendly Web Sites

When typing the address of a Web site, begin with www, then type in the name of the site. Type it in carefully or you may end up in the wrong place. Some sites have long addresses so you'll need to take your time and be careful. If you mess up and end up in the wrong site, you can always hit the Back button and try again.

Our list of sites is designed to give you examples of some of the better sites on the Internet that are designed for kids. Some are fun and others are educational. Actually, the sites with a lot of information have plenty of cool stuff about subjects that you may just happen to be interested in, even if you're not doing homework. There is nothing wrong with looking at a Web site about boats, elephants, or spaghetti, although it's not likely that you'll find one with a picture of an elephant on a boat eating spaghetti. But, you never know . . .

Since there are so many cool Web sites out there, we've listed some of the more popular ones. We've also tried to give you one or two examples of sites on many different subjects. There are many sites on animals but we selected just a few. The Bronx Zoo site, for instance, is a great example of a Web site about animals. Certainly the sites from the San Diego Zoo or the Philadelphia Zoo are probably just as interesting with pictures and lots of cool stuff about animals. We just couldn't list all the Web sites on a subject or you wouldn't be able to lift this book! Some of your favorite sites may have a section called Links, which shows a bunch of Web sites that they think are good (and are probably on the same topic).

We also tried to stay away from sites that are designed to sell you stuff. If Mom and or Dad says it's okay to shop online, you'll find many places where you can spend money. However, many parents may not think you need to do too much online

My Aching Eyes!

You are supposed to be sitting 15 to 18 inches back from the screen. Don't sit too close. And, if your eyes start getting tired, it's time to sign off and take a break. Your eyes are important, and there is nothing that you can't go back and find online later. Know when to take a rest.

shopping until you get a little older. Some of the sites that have fun and games also have a place where you can look at products they sell. It's not up to us to suggest you buy anything or not, sorry.

Next to each site you'll see E, F, or L.

An E stands for **educational**, meaning this is a great site for finding information to help with your homework or to learn something new.

An F stands for **fun**, which means that all kinds of activities including puzzles, mazes, quizzes, online games, crafts, chats, and or other fun activities can be found on the site. Some sites have them all!

L stands for **links**, which is a collection of other Web sites that you can go to. It's sort of like a book that has a reference section.

We've listed the main purpose or purposes of each

So, here are 70 sites you may want to check out. Some have links to other kid-friendly Web sites. We've noted the few that are not strictly designed for kids. Age ranges and level of difficulty will vary depending on the site and which part of it you click on to visit. Sometimes a site will be good if you are 8 or if you are 12 years old, depending on where you click. So, check them out.

Consider This

Wait! It Was There Yesterday

Sites change. Some sites may not have "chat" one day. That doesn't mean that by the time you get this book, someone at that Web site won't have said, "Hey, let's add a chat room!" and just like that they have a chat room.

4CHILDREN.COM *www.4children.com* (**L**)—is a Web site that links to many other sites, for kids and for parents. The Fun Stuff and Kid's Clothes are shopping areas, so go to them with your mom or dad. Show and Tell has links to many great places like zoos and museums, while Book Nook has great stories. TV Shows & Channels hook you up with Web sites like Nickelodeon, PBS Kids, and Fox Kids. The Web Sites for Kids section leads to more fun places. It includes Yahooligans, which even has a search engine for kids! Also on the list is Super Snooper, a cool information finder. At Kids Edutainment, you can hook up with other kids online. There is also an Awesome Library, which has reviews of Web resources. If you're looking for lots of Web sites to check out, this site can help you find them.

ACME CITY *www.acmecity.com* (**F, L**)—is a place all you super-hero fans will definitely want to visit. This Web site has a page for Superman and one for Batman! You can read the history of each superhero, preview new books, or download cool pic-tures. Of course you can also e-mail other superhero fans and read and contribute to the message boards. The site links to DC COMICS, which is also a good place to read pages from comics even before they show up in the store! Click on Secret Files to learn more about your favorite heroes as well as the history of all the villains. You can even get a subscription to buy comics from this site, with permission from your parents.

ALLOWANCENET *www.allowancenet.com* (**E**)—is a place parents and kids can look at together to figure out how to set up and manage an allowance. You can get free stuff by earning spe-cial rewards. You can also learn about earning an allowance based on doing your chores. You have to sign up for this Web site, but it may be worth it. Whether or not you get an allowance, it's always good to learn about saving and earning money.

AMERICA ONLINE *www.aolgames.com* **(F)**—has a neat Web site for anyone who loves to play games. This is a site for kids and adults. You can read Games News or preview the hottest new games. You can even read a review of a game that you might be interested in buying. The site is updated weekly, so you won't read about old games. There are also tournaments where you play against other people and clubs you can join with Mom or Dad's permission. Once you register, you can play against kids from all over the world. If you are interested in a particular game, you can study the strategy guide and learn more about how to play. It would be impossible to list all the games available on this site. The categories include board games, card games, game shows, computer games, and word games. Don't be upset if a game seems too hard. There are games for all ages and all skill levels. You can start out with the easier ones, and as you get better you'll learn some of the harder games.

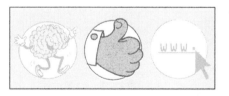

AMERICAN GIRL DOLLS *www.americangirl.com* **(F)**—has a Web site designed for those of you who collect these popular dolls. One part of the site is for shopping and the other part is for fun. The fun section includes a To Do Today area, a Paper Doll area, a place to meet and read about Real American Girls, an area that lets you send out cards called E-Card Express, a place called Puzzle Play, and a section for stories. Much of the material on the site comes from other girls who are fans of the popular dolls.

THE AMERICAN LIBRARY ASSOCIATION
www.ala.org/ICONN/kcfavorites.html **(E, L)**—has several Web sites. One site lists all the Web sites that school librarians agree are the most helpful for students from kindergarten through high school. The sites are listed by subjects: general curriculum, animals, art, astronomy, biographies, chemistry, earth science, environment/ecology, geography, government, history, holidays, language arts, math, reference, science, social studies, and others. There is also a question-and-answer section.

ASK DR. MATH *www.askdrmath.com* **(E)**—is a great site to visit if you need help with your math homework. You can also use it if you just like doing things with numbers—honest! There are examples and answers to questions for students from kindergarten through college. From questions and answers on negative numbers right up to the concept of infinity, you'll find anything related to math, even geometry, fractions, square roots, and math history. There are also math puzzles, projects, and problems. You can even ask Dr. Math a question. Dr. Math just sits around all day with special calculators and special "math machines" waiting for a challenge! Whether it's for homework or just a chance to put on your thinking cap and exercise that brain of yours, Dr. Math is a site worth visiting.

ASK JEEVES FOR KIDS *www.ajkids.com* **(E)**—is the place to go if you need homework help or just want to find out more about a subject. You can ask a question or choose from some commonly asked questions on any number of topics. Jeeves is hooked up to Web sites that cover all sorts of information from classic books you may be reading for English class to information on the NASA space shuttles. Jeeves also has an advice section, information for teachers, and listings of educational TV

Same Site?

John and Jonah think they have both navigated to the same Web site. But one of the sites has been updated! Can you find the 13 differences between these two home pages?

shows. Jeeves has a fun side too. There is even a place to ask where to find the best games. Check Jeeves out if you're "looking for the 411" (information, that is).

You can also tell Mom and Dad that there is an Ask Jeeves Web site for grown-ups, too. (Do you know who the character Jeeves is? He is a brainy butler who constantly saves his boss and his friends from embarrassing situations in the books of novelist P. G. Wodehouse.)

BIG BREW *www.bigbrew.com* (**F**)—has created a different kind of Web site. This site may not be very colorful or have cool characters, but it is very challenging. Fifth graders around the country voted it one of their favorite sites. When you first enter its home page, you will be able to choose from Fun Things, Games, AVI Movies (which won't work on some computers without certain software), or Different Things. Each section will lead you to a list of awesome activities. Each one has to be downloaded first. In Meeses.exe, you use a dart gun to shoot little mice that run all over your screen. Don't be surprised if they seek revenge.

If you are interested in how the brain works, you can play Brain.exe (for kids 10 and over). This game asks a series of questions about how you see things. Once you answer them, you can read the evaluation of your answers and learn more about the brain. You can also select Slugfest.exe and punch out David Letterman! AVI films are short films you can download and view. This is a very interactive and unique site.

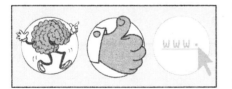

BONUS.COM *www.bonus.com* (**E, F**)—is a bonus for game lovers. The site has tons of games including sports games, monster games, brain games, playoff games, and word games. The best part is they're easy to play. Most of the games are great fun, but you will find a few duds. For some games the biggest challenge is figuring out how to play, because some of the instructions are in other languages. New versions of old games like Othello (using frogs' heads on the pieces) are fun, but a bad version of Ms. Pacman leaves something to be desired. One of the best things about these games is that you don't need to download anything special to play most of them.

There is also a What's Cookin' section with plenty of recipes. A News section has the latest on what's going on. And a Showtime section is loaded with quizzes and information about your favorite pop stars from Will Smith to Sabrina to the Backstreet Boys. The Illusions section has a host of magic tricks, lessons on how to juggle, optical illusions, and much more. A Fashion section teaches you about different types of fashion throughout history and even gives you some lessons on how to make your own clothes. The bottom line it that Bonus.com is loaded with things to do and things to learn about. You can spend hours looking at this site!

THE BRONX ZOO *www.bronxzoo.com* (E, F)—provides a wonderful site for children and adults. It's the next best thing to actually visiting this world-famous zoo. You can look at the Animals page or click on Kids Only to enter a great part of this Web site. A page called Wild Arcade is chock-full of games. You also have the rare opportunity to get involved in saving wild animals and learning how to protect their environment by joining Conservation Kids. Wild Animal Facts will teach you all you ever wanted to know about many types of wild animals. This is a great site for anyone who loves animals and can't get out to the zoo as often as they would like.

Sometimes it takes a long time for a picture to appear on your computer screen. Color in all the triangles to see what picture you have gotten from the "We Love Arachnids" Web site.

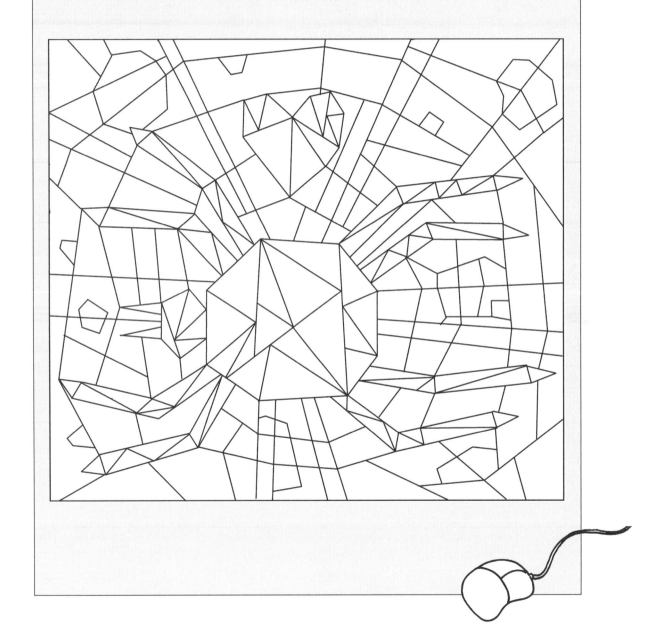

THE BUTTERFLY WEB SITE *www.butterflywebsite.com* (E)—has an amazing amount of information about butterflies. A section called Public Gardens tells you where to find butterflies all over the world. Most interesting is the photo gallery with pictures of all kinds of butterflies. Basically you can find anything you could possibly want to know about these fabulous flying creatures along with information on other insects as well.

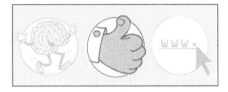

CANDYSTAND *www.candystand.com* (F)—is a colorful Web site brought to you by Nabisco, a company that makes crackers, cookies, and candy like LifeSavers. Just so you won't forget about their candy, most games have names like Breath Savers Billiards, Bubble Yum Foul Shot Shoot-Out, Fruit Stripe Yipes Hang Gliding Adventure, and Ice Breakers Ultimate Bobsled. There are over 40 games, ranging from a unique photo safari game to a more typical TV trivia game. There are even card games like solitaire and poker. You'll need to download Shockwave to play the games. If you don't have it, you can find it at the Candystand Toolbox. What's extra special about these games is that you can win real prizes like a DVD player, Sega Dreamcast, or a gift certificate, which is like cash for a store. The colorful site has become very popular. There is also information on candy, including commercials you can play back, and an area where you can create and send your own animated greeting cards. Yes, you can even order candy.

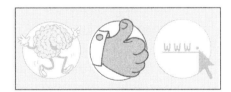

CARTOON NETWORK *www.cartoonnetwork.com* (F)—has a Web site with lots of links to information about their huge library of cartoon favorites. From brand-new cartoons to short movies, there is plenty to keep you busy as you bop around the home site for Scooby-Doo, Dexter, Space Ghost, Johnny Bravo, and even those Powerpuff Girls. You can go behind the scenes to learn how cartoons are made or you can download games to play. There are video clips and artwork from other kids, plus schedules and highlights from the cartoons. This is one of those sites you can just keep looking through, particularly if you enjoy the many classic and original cartoons on the popular network.

THE CASE.COM FOR KIDS *www.thecase.com/kids/* (**F**)—is a great site if you like mysteries and magic. You can solve mysteries, or write your own or learn some magic tricks. You can also talk to other mystery fans. There is a special link to one of the all-time favorite mystery series, Nancy Drew, with original online stories and games. This is the only thing you'll have to download. You can join TheCase.com/kidsclub and buy books, but you'll have to talk with Mom or Dad before you can buy or join anything. Learning with Mysteries and Lesson Plans are two other areas that are really more for grown-ups. You can also go right to the Kids Love a Mystery part of the Web site by typing in *www.kidsloveamystery.com*.

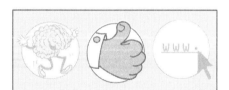

CHEF BOYARDEE *www.chefboy.com* (**F**)—the long-time king of Spaghetti-O's has a Web site with arcade games, a place to make your own TV commercial, and a place to make comics. The games are cool, but you'll need to make sure you have the software to play them. There are Comix and a Pasta Club that you can join. You can even read the story of Chef Boyardee.

CHILDREN'S BUTTERFLY SITE *www.mesc.usgs.gov* (**E**)—is a terrific and beautiful site designed by the Midcontinental Ecological Science Center. Anyone who is fascinated by these colorful creatures will definitely love this site. There are Coloring Pages that have outlines of butterflies to color in and a description of the butterflies pictured. Another page is for frequently asked questions about butterflies and moths. If you want to learn more, you can click on Books and Videos for plenty of references. The best part is the fabulous collection of photographs of butterflies from all over the world that can be viewed by going to the Gallery. This site is very enjoyable (and beautiful) and a very good place to learn more about butterflies.

THE CIA HOMEPAGE FOR KIDS *www.cia.gov/cia* **(E, F)**—is a Web site that all future spies and secret agents will not want to miss. To find it, you need to sign on to *www.cia.gov/cia* and then click on CIA's Home Page for Kids. If you go into What We Do, you can learn all about what the Central Intelligence Agency does and who they are. The section marked CIA Seal has a picture of the CIA's official seal and describes what each part of it means. You can also learn all about the history of the CIA. If you choose CIA Canine Corps, you'll learn how dogs are trained (as spy dogs) to work with the agency. You can even hear one bark.

Unlike some of the other sites designed by the U.S. government, this one has some real cool games and trivia quizzes. If you click on Geography, your monitor will show you a map of the world to test your geography skills. In the Games section, you'll find an awesome decoding game called Code Warriors and a fun game called Try a Disguise. By the time you are finished visiting this site, you'll be thinking up your own disguises and buying an official "spy" trench coat!

COLORING.COM *www.coloring.com* **(F)**—is an online coloring book. You can choose from a large variety of animal, holiday, and sport pictures. You can even e-mail your drawings to your friends or relatives. The pictures can be printed out on a color printer to hang up on the refrigerator or you can print out the pages and color them in later.

CONJUROR.COM *www.conjuror.com/magictricks/* **(F)**—is a terrific Web site if you want to learn magic tricks to dazzle your friends and family. The Challenge Knot Tie (a rope trick), the Mysterious Coin Balance, and the famous Self-Tying Handkerchief can all be part of your magic act. The Conjuror Archives contain a lot of information about the history of magic, including the discovery of witchcraft and the writings of the greatest escape artist of all time, Harry Houdini. There are also links to Card Trick Central and to a product review section that can give you the scoop on magic items before you go out and spend your allowance on them. There's even a jugglers' link.

COOLMATH *www.coolmath.com* **(E)**—is the place to go for math homework help and more. All right, so it may not be as exciting as the "fun and games" sites, but if you need help understanding math, this is a great place to learn about algebra, geometry, and calculus. The site also offers math games and puzzles . . . and they're not easy! From kids to adults, these math puzzles will test and torture you. If you like math games, check it out; and be patient, you may need to sit and think about these for a while. There are also links to tons of other math sites that include just about anything your teacher can throw your way.

COOLTOONS *www.cooltoons.com* **(F)**—is a must-see Web site for all Rugrats fans. You can meet the characters and take part in an interactive adventure. You can also print pictures or color online. If you loved *The Rugrats Movie*, you will want to learn all about how it was made or play a memory game. There is even a guide for the new episodes, including never-before-seen pictures. The Angelica Pie Throwing Game is a fun Shockwave activity that lets you throw pies at Angelica, and who hasn't wanted to do that? This game has three levels of difficulty, so all kids can play. There are also other games on the site and fun stuff about other cartoons such as *The Wild Thornberrys*.

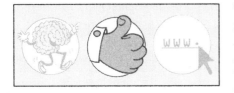

CRAYOLA.COM *www.crayola.com* **(F)**—is the Web site of the makers of Crayola crayons. Rather than just sell you crayons, they offer a lot to do. A large Crafts Central area shows you how to make paper people, animals, puppets, designs, and other things that you can print and color in. You can also find crayon facts, trivia, history, and information about great artists like Leonardo da Vinci and Michelangelo (neither of whom used crayons in their work). The games section has download-able games (you may have to wait a while for these to down-load) and there is a story room. You can also find puzzles, pictures, and greeting cards to print out and color. No, you can't color online, but why would they want you to do that anyway—after all, they make crayons.

CYBER ZOOMOBILE *www.primenet.com/~brendel/index.html* **(E, L)**— is one of the best places to find information on all sorts of ani-mals. Lots of pictures are on the home page, which lets you click to get facts and more photos about your favorite creatures. Besides being a great place for homework help (particularly when you have a report to do), the Cyber Zoomobile has links to a great number of the world's zoos and animal parks, animal trivia, brain teasers to test your animal knowledge, and much more. If you love animals, this is a perfect place to check out.

DICTIONARY.COM *www.dictionary.com* **(E, F, L)**—is exactly what it says it is, and more. For English class, writing assignments, and expanding your vocabulary (not to mention much-needed spelling help), Dictionary.com can be of service. You can ask Doctor Dictionary for the meaning of a word. You can also play word search games, try your hand at crossword puzzles, find similar words in Roget's Thesaurus, learn more about writing style and word usage, get questions answered about grammar (yuck!), or click to link to newspapers or classic texts. This site is a general site, so don't be surprised if the crossword puzzles (from *Dell Crossword Puzzles*) are a bit hard. You may need some help with the words on the site, so feel free to ask Mom or Dad to look with you. There is even a place where you can translate words from English into other languages.

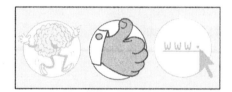

DISNEY *www.disney.com* **(F)**—as you would probably expect, Disney has several wonderful Web sites. They are colorful and musical and have many different things to see, play, and learn. If you go to Disney.com, be prepared to stay for a while. The home page can lead you to a wide variety of places. For example, if you click on Zeether you can then enter the Games section where you can play all types of games including sports, strategy, or action games. You can also join competitions with other players. If you click on Activities, you can choose Arts and Crafts, Paint, or go to a special Print Center.

Back on the home page, there are many more choices. Send-a-Card will give you a choice of greeting cards for all occasions. The cards all have Disney characters on them; some have music. Conduct a Symphony is great fun, but you do need Macromedia Shockwave 7.0. Have no fear, Disney will help you download it. If you want to shop (with Mom or Dad), you can see what's available at the Disney Store. You can also help plan your family vacation to—where else—Disney World or on a Disney Cruise. One of the most interesting categories is called Disney A-Z. Here you can either explore Disney history by visiting the Disney Museum and Archives or you can test your Disney IQ by taking a trivia quiz. Check out the Behind the Scenes section, where you can learn how the Disney magic is made. If you are a Disney movie fan, click on Movies & Videos and find out what is currently in the theaters. In fact, you can even purchase tickets (with Mom and Dad, of course). There are games, places to chat, and more. There is a similar page for Disney TV shows. The possibilities are endless, so have some Disney fun. But, just like when you go to Disney World, don't try to do everything in one day!

EPLAY *www.eplay.com* (**E, F**)—is a free educational Internet site for kids ages 8 to 13. You can find homework help, use online activity workbooks, look at World Almanacs for kids, and even play some games. One section lets you play Net Detectives and track down evil Internet villains. The site is designed for parents and teachers as well as kids, so click on Kids at the bottom of the home page. One really cool thing is that you can create your own page where you can save your scores on the games or link to other sites. You can also get homework assignments or class notes from your teachers right at home. You need to join to participate, but it is free.

FLEETKIDS *www.fleetkids.com* (**E, F**)—is a place to play games while you develop your money spending and saving skills. No, real money is not involved, but there are several games that will let you make money decisions. If you want to show how smart you can be with your allowance, this is the place to practice. You'll find information on how to create a budget so you will know how much you are spending. You'll also learn how to set goals so you will know how much you will be saving for something you really want in the future. You need to sign up to play, or be signed up with Headbone Zone. Games include Money Matic, Price Tag, and Chunka Change. You can also sign up to win prizes for your school.

FOX KIDS *www.foxkids.com* **(F)**—is a promotional site that features some downloadable games and information and schedules of Fox Kids programming. If you love those cute Digital Monsters, this is also the official Digimon site. When you get to the opening page, click on the icon, Official Digimon Site, in the upper-right corner. You'll enter a place where you can learn facts about your favorite Digi or see video clips from the show. There is also information on the Power Rangers, plus contests you can enter and a Fox Kids Club you can join. To enter contests or join the club, ask Mom or Dad. You can also click on a place that has action, adventure, and sports games plus brainteasers and more. The animation lab will teach you how to draw characters and learn all about cartoons. You'll even see a Boyz Channel, a Girlz Channel, and a place for Blockheads (a game like Tetris that you don't need any downloads to play). There are jokes, fun facts, and other things on this rather large Web site.

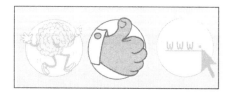

FREEZONE *www.freezone.com* **(F)**—Where Kids Connect, is a place to answer quizzes about (or find other fun things relating to) the latest trends from Pokémon to Harry Potter to Britney Spears in the Pop Culture section. There are also polls about things that are going on in the world. You can chat in the chat rooms, post messages on any of a number of bulletin boards, and send postcards. There are even "junior jobs" available online. You can get advice from other kids or check out the Fun and Games section with puzzles, fantasy sports, jokes, scrambles, and other things to do. It's an all-around good time site that lets you interact and get involved or just settle back and play games or read what other kids have to say.

A lot of Web sites want to hear your opinion about the things you like. Ask a parent or friend to help you complete this online review of a new movie. IMPORTANT: Don't let the other person see the review. Just tell them the kind of words needed to fill in each blank. Then write the words they give you in the spaces provided. When you've filled in all the blanks, read your review together!

"_____ Monkey" is a really funny movie. The main
   (ADJECTIVE)

character is a _____ monkey named _____ .
            (ADJECTIVE)   (SILLY NAME)

He lives _____ in a _____ cave in
      (ADVERB)   (ADJECTIVE)

_____ . After _____ eats a
(COUNTRY NAME)   (SAME SILLY NAME)

_____ _____ , he turns into a _____
(ADJECTIVE)   (NOUN)   (ADJECTIVE)

_____ _____ monster who tries _____
(ADJECTIVE)   (COLOR)   (VERB ENDING IN -ING)

_____ . The movie ends _____ ,
(NAME OF A US STATE CAPITOL)   (ADVERB)

and is a _____ surprise!
       (ADJECTIVE)

MOVIE RATING: _____ stars
               (BIG NUMBER)

Use a simple substitution code (A = Z, B = A, C = B, D = C, etc.) to figure out which web site has this strange address. Connect the numbered dots and the lettered dots to find a silly picture!

address in code:

xxx.gjtizebodf.dpn

real address:

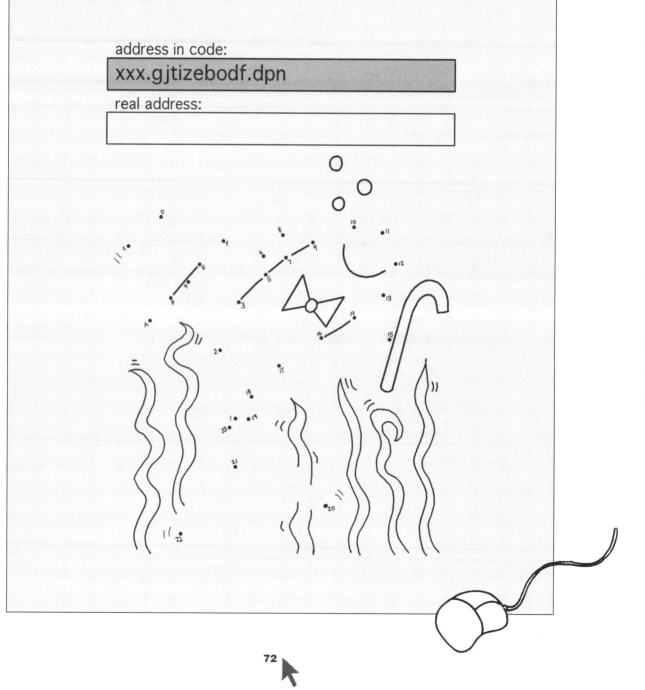

72

FUNBRAIN *www.funbrain.com* (**E, F**)—is a great site where you can have fun and learn all at once. There are many games to choose from. You must click on your age and then you will have a list of choices that includes Numbers, Words, Universe, Culture, or Extra. This is a great way to get extra practice in any of these subjects while having fun. For example, you can practice math with Math Baseball, brush up on your grammar with Grammar Gorillas, or work on your spelling by clicking on Spellaroo. Games range from kindergarten level through eighth grade. There are a tremendous number of games and activities for all ages.

FUNOLOGY *www.funology.com* (**F**)—is a colorful site with games like Find the Dinosaur and something called Brain Drain that features mind challengers. Boredom Buster activities include holiday crafts. You can learn easy magic tricks Abracadabra, riddles in Tummy Tickler, and easy-to-follow recipes in In The Kitchen. It's an easy-to-navigate Web site that is not over-whelming and is updated often.

FUNSCHOOL *www.funschool.com* (**E, F**)—is a very popular site for kids from preschool through the sixth grade. It offers new and updated activities on a regular basis. Browser the Bus takes viewers through different educational games. Math and geography games are available for kids in the third through sixth grades. The menu lets you choose the right place by grade. Games and activities are updated often so you won't get bored playing the same ones again and again.

HAMSTERDANCE *www.hamsterdance.com* (**F**)—is just plain silly. But make sure your speakers are on and check it out, even if it's only for a few minutes. Then tell your friends to check it out too. There just aren't many sites like this one—which is probably a good thing. You can also check out fishydance.com, cow-dance.com, and other dancing animals from the makers of this comical site.

HARPER CHILDRENS *www.harperchildrens.com* **(E, F)**—is the HarperCollins Publishers' Web site for kids. It's one of the better sites from book publishing companies. Besides looking at some of the latest books for children, you can create your own animals or robots at Switcheroos. There are eight wacky word stories (like Madlibs) where you can create a silly story by filling in a bunch of words that end up in all the wrong places in your story . . . you'll see. There are word jumbles and a section where you will find plenty of activities, including crafts.

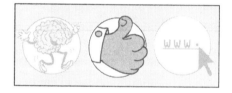

HBO4KIDS *www.hbo4kids.com* **(F)**—offers more than just stuff about HBO TV shows. You can build an action hero or a beast, or download and play games, or go to The Big Deal, which lets you state your opinions on a number of current subjects. Time Warp 7 has characters that take part in stories (some stories are historical, like Paul Revere's Ride or the Boston Tea Party). You can click on the part of the story you want to read next. Gross Goodies has favorite recipes while Do It Yourself lists ideas of things to do, like fun jobs. And yes, there is some information on all the HBO kids' shows, including Paddington Bear and Babar.

HEADBONE ZONE *www.headbonezone.com* **(F, L)**—bills themselves as a site full of chat, games, e-mails, prizes, and more. And they are right! You can find a bunch of cool chat rooms, but kids under 13 need permission to enter. Rooms are monitored to make sure they remain fun. Headbone Zone has kids' rooms, teen rooms, theme rooms, and game rooms. There can be as many as 240 people chatting at once! You can also send messages to friends who are on the site.

There are also plenty of games to choose from, but these are the "mind game" variety for the over-12 group. You can cast your vote in polls on "hot" subjects, find out what astrological sign you are, or share a joke. It's a very busy, very popular Web site that is almost like landing on a different planet. In other words, it takes some getting used to. After a couple of visits or some help from a friend who's already into "The Zone," you'll get the hang of the site and start playing games, chatting, and hanging out there. You can even search the Web, in a manner of speaking, by Asking Jeeves. (Ask Jeeves is another site (see page 58), where you can get questions answered.) Enjoy Headbone Zone, but please don't overdo it.

KELLOGG'S *www.kelloggs.com* (F)—sponsors a Web site that is full of games, puzzles, and activities as well as some really cool screensavers that you can download. One activity is called Swirl Safari, which offers loads of neat mazes. You will need to register to play. If you are under 13, you will need to ask a parent to help you. Incredible Shrinking Jacks has some optical illusions that are excellent. But don't go here before eating, because it might make you hungry. Kellogg's displays their cereals throughout the site!

KIDNEWS *www.kidnews.com* (E)—is written by kids. There are many categories. Creative Writing features stories and poems. At News, you can talk about what is going on in the headlines. Reviews is the place to put up your review of a book or movie. In Sports, you can read or write about teams or players you love. And there's even a place for short hello messages to friends or pen pals. There is also a Cool Hangout area that links to a lot of writing sites for kids and teens. In Goodies, you can look at a list of school magazines and creative story magazines. If you like reading what other kids have to say or if you want your story, poem, review, or other writing to appear on the Internet, this is the place.

KIDS CLICK! *http://sunsite.berkeley.edu/kidsclick!/* **(E, L)**—is a search engine filtered for kids with loads of information. You can search by categories, which include Facts/Current Events, Science & Math, The Arts, Popular Entertainment, Weird & Mysterious, Literature, Computers/The Internet, and others. You can also search for subjects by their first letter or just type in what you're looking for. The site is easy to use and won't give you tons of other Web sites that are not on the subject you want.

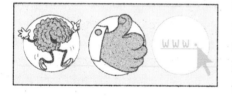

KIDSCOM *www.kidscom.com* **(E, F)**—is an entertaining electronic playground for kids of all ages. The home page gives you five main choices. At Around The World, you can actually be heard by presidents or other world leaders in a section called Voice to the World. Let them know how you feel about things. At On Location, you can learn about kids from all over the world. There are tons of games and activities including kid-created sites. Make New Friends allows you to meet other kids who have similar hobbies or interests. Then there is Kids Talk About, where you can vote on and voice your opinions on issues or write a story. Just For Fun is just what you would expect—great games and fun. Cool Stuff is all about new products and services for kids. You'll learn ways to earn Kidskash Points that you can cash in for prizes! KidsCom also has a place for parents and teachers.

KIDS DOMAIN *www.kidsdomain.com* **(F, L)**—is one of those sites you could spend a day or three checking out. There is a ton of stuff here and the opening menu is very "user friendly" (easy to use). Before you know it, you'll find fun stuff to do! There are plenty of games (check with your parents before downloading them), a newsletter, a Pokémon activity page, and loads of crafts and contests. There's even a place where you can get information about computer books and software that will help you learn much more about computers—even how to program one. Kids Domain also has a search engine as well as links to other sites. Click on Holidays for lots of information, quizzes, clip art, games, mazes, crafts, and software relating to all the major holidays. Icons has tons of tiny icons that are really cool. Remember, icons are those little pictures that you click on that take you to a link. These icons don't lead to any sites. They are designed as artwork. You'll find Barbie icons, Muppet icons, superhero icons, Pokémon icons, and many more!

KIDSITES.COM *www.kidsites.com* (**E, F, L**)—has listings of kid-friendly, kid-approved sites. It's a great place to find educational sites about animals, art, dinosaurs, history, math, music, science, or space. You'll also find fun sites with activities, coloring, comics, crafts, online games, sports information, storybooks, and lots more. There are reviews of new and featured sites, plus articles for Mom and Dad about getting the most out of the Web and helping you find your way around.

KIDSSPACE *www.kidsspace.com* (**F**)—is a great site for kids who love their Grandma or don't have a Grandma. It is a Web site where you can e-mail all sorts of questions and she will answer them as soon as she can. As she says, "I'm a little old and slow, please be patient and come back soon." Grandma also shares some of her favorite recipes (including her recipe for chocolate chip cookies). In the Story Time area, you can e-mail Grandma your favorite story or read one of hers. Grandpa also has a page on this site. He knows all about fishing, sports, and fixing things. You can join an e-mail list by sending your first name, the state or country you live in, your age, and three things you enjoy. An area called Fun Things for Kids To Do links to Crafts from

Disney's *family.com* site. You can also choose "Rader's Interactive Space Exploration-Center, which is a wonderful astronomy site where you can explore the solar system.

LYCOS KIDS ZONE *www.lycoszone.com* **(E)**—has games and a homework zone. The games are primarily for kids under seven, but the Homework Zone helps kids from kindergarten through sixth grade. You can use a Kids Almanac, encyclopedia, dictionary, atlas, or an awesome directory of animals. The site is easy to navigate, and you will find plenty of help with all those tough subjects like math, science, and history.

MAJOR LEAGUE BASEBALL *www.majorleaguebaseball.com or www.majorleaguebaseball.com/u/baseball/mlbcom/kids/* **(F)**—has its own official Web site with areas for anything and everything about the Big Leagues. There are tons of sports sites out there, but this one is loaded with stories, the latest baseball news, statistics, schedules, photos, baseball history, and even a section for kids. The kids' section lets you read about your favorite ballplayers or get tips on playing the game. You can ask baseball-related questions and get answers, or just send an e-mail to your favorite player. Kids and grown-ups can find plenty to keep them busy on this site if they love the game of baseball.

MAKING FRIENDS *www.makingfriends.com* **(F)**—is a wonderful Web site if you enjoy making things like jewelry, bead projects, or paper dolls, or doing any number of crafts. You can even learn how to make Pokémon crafts. It is a great place to get ideas for birthday or holiday gifts. This site has a mailing list, so you can get e-mail when there are new projects. You'll also enjoy making friends as you meet other kids who have the

How-To

Wrong Address?

Sometimes you've typed in the address correctly, but the site cannot be found. Strange, isn't it? It may mean that the site is no longer available or there may be a problem connecting with it. The problem can be caused by the Web site (maybe the people who run it are busy working on it). It may also be caused by your computer or your Internet connection. Try it again later. Sometimes if you try a different search engine, you can find the site. If you search with Microsoft Explorer but the site didn't register with them, then they can't find it. You can add the home pages of a few search engines—Yahoo!, Excite, Lycos, and others—to access easily.

same interest in crafts. It's a lot of fun, and you'll learn to make some great stuff.

MAMAMEDIA *www.mamamedia.com* **(L)**—is a very cool site because it links to more than two thousand kid-friendly sites. MaMaMedia has a tremendous selection of games and projects. You can also surf the Web here or e-mail other kids. If you click on Zap, you can design your own MaMaMedia screen. There are three other categories, too. Surprise links to game and activity sites. Romp is a cool place to surf. Buzz is a good place to connect with other kids and share ideas.

MARY-KATE AND ASHLEY *www.marykateandashley.com* **(F)**—the Olsen twins are growing up and now they have a Web site of their own. The adventurous teens are still making movies, and their site is primarily a way to promote their latest films and videos. If you are a fan, there are plenty of photos, frequently asked questions, and lots of information on this very popular Web site.

MCDONALDS *www.mcdonalds.com* **(F)**—where all kids love to eat, also has a fun Web site. There is a page designed for young kids called Hey Kids McDonaldland. There is also an online coloring book and a place where you can listen to some McDonalds, commercial jingles. If you go to Fun Stuff, you can take a stroll through Fry Kids Forest and play some cool games. There are matching games that test your concentration skills and a place to test your memory and knowledge in the McDonaldland Time Machine. McWorld is definitely for older kids. It is loaded with games, polls, and other fun things to do. For example, when playing Sauce Slat, you can shoot different types of sauces at chicken nuggets. It is fun, but it may also make you hungry!

MOOCOW *www.moocow.com* (**E, F**)—is for all you cow lovers. If the sound of cows is moo-sic to your ears, you'll enjoy the welcoming moo and have fun with cow quizzes, connect-the-dots games, and plenty of fun recipes. You can even browse the cow store. There's even an illustrated story of milk. No, it's not a moo-vie, but it explains how milk comes from a cow and ends up on your cereal. There are frequently asked dairy questions and a contest that asks you to tell what you think cows are thinking. The site isn't packed, but it's fun and educational for a short visit.

NATIONAL WILDLIFE FEDERATION *www.nwf.org* (**E, F**)—has a lot of information for grownups. But in the Kids Zone, you can find their Games page with riddles and Match'em. In the Cool Tours section, you can take a virtual tour of wetlands or study endangered species. The Earth Savers page is for kids nine and older. You can join a club or program and receive e-mail and newsletters (ask Mom or Dad before signing up). This is a very cool thing to do because you can help save some of the many endangered animals. Ranger Rick is for kids under nine. There you can draw colorful pictures of animals and play games. Also, if you are looking for campgrounds or a summer camp, go to More Fun for help.

NICK JR. *www.nickjr.com* (**F**)—has weekly games and information on Nickelodeon's shows and printouts for younger kids. There are many fun activities for older kids as well. When you first arrive at the home page, a menu lists many of the shows at the bottom of the screen. Once you choose one, you can download a game and play. Some of the games need Shockwave to load. You can also view great pictures of popular Nick characters or listen to the theme songs from some of your favorite shows.

NICKELODEON *www.nick.com* **(F)**—offers a very busy Web site with many options. You can check out information on new film releases, look up your favorite shows, or see what the TV stars are doing. From the main page, you can look at the channel's programs and get fun facts and pictures about the shows, including *Rugrats*, *Hey Arnold*, and even *The Brady Bunch* (which also shows up on the Nick at Night site). There are games (that need to be downloaded), plus trivia, online polls, and lots of fun stuff. You can also get the schedule of Nickelodeon shows and link to other Nick sites like Nick Jr., Nick at Night, Nick G and S (a games and sports site), Nick Noggin (a learning site), and Red Rocket (Nickelodeon's online toy store).

NINTENDO *www.nintendo.com* **(F)**—has a Web site that reviews their latest games for computers and for Game Boy. Along with the information on the latest games, you can look at a list of previously released games to see which ones you don't have. You will also find an FAQ (frequently asked questions) section, a few fun word scrambles, and crossword puzzles. The site also lists links to other Nintendo-related Web sites.

NOT JUST FOR KIDS *www.night.net/kids* **(E, F, L)**—is a great place to choose some of the best sites for kids. Rosie's Rhubarb Review lists and links to many interesting sites by category. For example if you click on Interesting Places, you will get a terrific list of sites about interesting places to visit like Canada Stamps, Martin Luther King, Jr., Today-in-History, and Net Trek Cafe. Many of these sites link to others. Another selection from Rosie's table is Music and Radio. It allows you access to Walt Disney Records Web site or Judy and David OnLine, where everyone gets to sing and enjoy this online songbook. Not Just for Kids is a wonderful starting place that leads to many other fun sites.

PETCO *www.petco.com* (E, F)—has a great Web site for all the animal lovers in cyberspace. You can learn all about how to care for your pets. You can also join the P.A.L.S. club (with an okay from Mom or Dad) and receive extra savings in the PETCO stores. If you click on PetPourri, you can draw pictures of your favorite pets and write stories about them. There are coloring pages for kids and some interesting information about different kinds of pets. You can also ask an expert any animal-care questions you might have.

ROUTE 6-16 *www.cyberpatrol.com/616* (L)—is a Web search engine designed for kids by Cyberpatrol and The Learning Company. It's really simple to use. Just type in whatever you are looking for and you will get eight to 10 places to look. This is a great place to search for homework help or to look up stuff just for fun.

SEA WORLD/BUSCH GARDENS *www.seaworld.org* (F)—is the place to visit if you are interested in setting up an aquarium or learning more about whales, dolphins, manatees, or gorillas. The site is designed for kids eight and older. It offers an amazing amount of information, photos, movie clips, reading lists, and an interactive question-and-answer area. If you have a Microsoft NetShow Player, you will be able to view the Shark.Cam and see live shots of the sharks at Sea World Florida.

SIKIDS *www.sikids.com* (F)—is the Web site from *Sports Illustrated For Kids* magazine. They offer a trivia contest with an outer space theme (who knows why), plus original cartoons, and polls where you can cast your own vote for awards like the NFL rookie of the year or NHL MVP. There are sports stories, places to give your opinion on sports, and some really neat sports star puzzles that range from easy to nearly impossible. It's a great place for sports fans.

SIMONSAYSKIDS *www.simonsays.com* **(E, F)**—is the Web site from book publishers Simon & Schuster. Click on Simonsayskids. Besides a look at some of the many books for children, you can go to the games section and check out the Cool Stuff. There are polls, quizzes, information on the Rugrats and other favorites, plus word finding and Madlibs types of games. It is one of many sites from book publishers where you can have fun and (with your parents) sit and look at some of the books you can order.

SNAPPLE *www.snapple.com* **(F)**—has a great Web site for anyone who likes to play video games. The best game on this site is called Good Fruit!, Bad Fruit!, which works a lot like Mario Brothers, using the keyboard to move your fruit around the board. You even get to choose your fruit, either Strawberry Sweetheart or Peachie Keen. There are also cool hunts and contests, and if you are lucky you can win Snapple.

SPACEDAY *www.spaceday.com* **(E, F)**—is an award-winning Web site. It is dedicated to Space Day, which is the Thursday before the anniversary of President Kennedy's 1961 challenge to "land a man on the Moon and return to the Earth." There are tons of related online events and activities. Try Destination Mars, for example. You must register to play. Once you enter, you are the captain of a ship on a virtual Mars mission. There are new episodes each week. You must complete one in order to go on to the next. It is awesome!

Or go into Mission Fun, where you'll find some exciting games like Planet Surfin' and Brain Warp. You will need to download Shockwave. Check out Friends of Space and send your friends and family an e-mail postcard from Mars or Jupiter. In The Phaser area, you'll learn all about the different phases of the Moon.

How-To

Here Come the Cops!

If you ever get a message on your computer screen telling you that the program has performed an illegal function, don't panic. You're not on your way to jail. It just means there has been a computer error. If you hit the X in the top right corner of the box with the message, sometimes it will go away. Other times, however, it will knock you offline and you will have to go back onto the Internet. You may even need to reboot, which is another way to say "restart" the computer. If in doubt about what to do or how to do it, ask a parent for help.

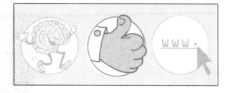

THUMB.COM *www.thumb.com* (F)—is just plain silly! Pictures and bios of thumbs with little wigs and clothes starring as all your *Star Wars* favorites in the movie Thumb Wars. It's worth checking out, even if all you do is shake your head and wonder how and why someone came up with all this nonsense.

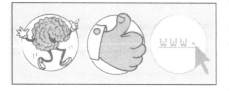

VOLCANO WORLD *www.volcano.und.nodak.edu/* (E, F)—is the perfect place to do research for that paper you are writing about volcanoes. It actually has more than you could ever need on the subject, plus neat photos and even movie clips of volcanoes in action. There is information on the latest eruptions. A volcanologist (someone who studies volcanoes) answers tons of questions. Volcano Adventures gives stories about volcanoes. And there are listings of volcanoes worldwide. Kids Door is an area with everything from virtual field trips to quizzes, games, and puzzles. You can even post your own volcano art or look at the pictures posted by other kids.

WARNER BROTHERS *www.kids.warnerbros.com* (F)—has a terrific Web site with lots of awesome stuff to look at and a tremendous amount of activities. With the right downloads, you can view clips from Warner Brothers movies like *Batman Beyond*. If you click on Web Cards, you can send a card by e-mail to a friend with a picture of your favorite character on it. You can play cool games in Looney Tunesville or visit Games & Arcade, where you can play a variety of neat games like Hot Dog Toss. You can even try to catch the Road Runner (beep beep!). Jack Frost is an especially *cool* place because you can build a virtual snowman. There is also a special Scooby Doo home page with more fun things to do. Of course, The Flintstones have their own Bedrock Web page with games and activities. The best thing about this site is that even if you somehow get off the kids' pages, you can still find many great things to do. For example, you can go to the Cartoon Cinema and watch a full-length cartoon or play cartoon trivia.

WEEKLY READER *www.weeklyreader.com* **(E, F)**—is by the same people who publish the *Weekly Reader* newspapers that you started reading back in kindergarten. This is an interesting Web site that is worth checking out. The site can be geared for a parent, a teacher, or a kid. So first, you need to click on I'm a Kid, then select your grade level. For each grade, there are plenty of contests and polls. At News Busters you can take a quiz and find out how much you know about the news. You can participate in a Weekly Poll and see the results the following week. If you are a photography buff, then you won't want to miss the Mystery Photo Contest.

THE WHITE HOUSE FOR KIDS *www.whitehouse.gov* **(E)**—is one of many wonderful Web sites that the federal government has designed. Once you sign on to *www.whitehouse.gov*, select The White House for Kids. The home page has six categories to choose from:

1. Location gives you the exact address and location of the White House. You can also learn where other famous buildings in Washington, D.C. are located.
2. History takes you back in time and teaches you how the house was constructed and traces the story of each president's stay in the White House. You can learn about the different rooms and what they are used for. You'll find interesting facts and trivia here.
3. Our President is a place to learn all about the current president and the vice president and their husbands or wives. You can click on a photo of each one and get their biography.

4. White House Kids provides pictures, facts, and trivia about all the kids and grandchildren who have lived in the White House.

5. White House Pets gives you the scoop on the pets that have lived there.

6. Write the President is a very cool place because you can write directly to the president, the first lady, the vice president, or his wife by e-mail. Although there are no games or activities at this site, it is very interesting and can be a major help if you need information on the White House or the president for school.

YAHOOLIGANS *www.yahooligans.com* (E, F, L)—is a multifaceted Web site with many terrific links. Some links help you learn more about current events like Black History Month or the Chinese New Year celebration. The home page has six main areas:

1. Around the World teaches you about different countries, the types of foods in them, what holidays are celebrated, and more. It's also a great place to go for help with homework.

2. Arts & Entertainment offers many possibilities, including comics and animation.

3. Fashion has a page for girls and the television page gives you info on your favorite actors and actresses. You can also download photos.

4. Sports & Recreations contains everything you want to know about sports, including great pictures to download, sounds, and even videos.

5. Computers & Games has tons of online and video games to download and play. There is also a page where you can create computer-generated art.

6. Science & Nature lets you learn about the weather, visit museums, and see every type of dinosaur you can imagine. This is also a good place for homework help.

Of course there is also a Pokémon page on this very big, very popular site from Yahoo.

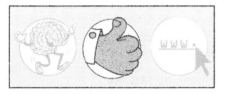

ZOOGDISNEY *www.zoogdisney.com* **(F)**—is another terrific Web site from the folks at Disney. This site is more interactive than Disney.com. It has more online activities and events. For example, if you click on Zeether Features and then on MZ's Music Zone, and then on In Concert, you can select from featured artists like Britney Spears or the Backstreet Boys and read their bios or try your hand at some trivia. You can also listen to their music and download pictures. Other choices in Zeether Features include The Magic Shop, Movie Surfers, and Bug Juice. They all have games and interactive adventures. If it's games you are looking for, just click on Twitch's Arcade. To play you must register, but by registering you will also gain access to the GO directory, a Disney search engine where you can look up Disney stuff. Once inside Twitch's Arcade, you can choose from a tremendous variety of games. If you are interested in meeting other kids or participating in polls or taking fun quizzes, then you can click on Express Yourself. There are lots of choices on this site that can keep you busy for hours.

www.fastlaughs

What is one sign that a computer is getting old?

Answer: It loses its memory!

FUN FACT

NASA, and More NASA

If you are wondering what else they do at NASA besides send up space shuttles and satellites, you can check out one of their many Web sites. Perhaps, that's what they are busy doing the rest of the time . . . making cool Web sites full of Space Age information. Besides the NASA page with its kids' section, NASA's Quest sites include Women of NASA, Space Team Online, Space Scientists Online, Mars Team Online, and many other sites on topics like the Hubble Telescope.

Government Sites

The federal government has designed many Web sites for kids. To access them, you often need to go to the Web site for the particular organization or department and then look for the kids' page. You can go to a search engine and type in "government Web sites for kids." That will bring up a list of many sites. Here are some of the more interesting sites, along with the addresses so you can find them:

Agriculture

www.usda.gov/news/usdakids/—USDA For Kids, from the National Agriculture Statistical Service and the Department of Agriculture

Crime and Law Enforcement

www.fbi.gov/kids/kids.htm—FBI Kids' and Youth Educational Page, from the Federal Bureau of Investigation

www.doj.gov/kidspage—Justice for Kids and Youth, from the Department of Justice

Environment and Nature

www.epa.gov/region7/kids/charlie.htm—Charlie's Corner, from the Environmental Protection Agency

www.usgs.gov/education/—The Learning Web, from the U.S. Geological Survey

www.niehs.nih.gov/kids/home.htm—National Institute of Environmental Health Sciences Kids' Page

Government

www.hud.gov/kids—Kids Next Door, from the Department of Housing and Urban Development

www.ustreas.gov/kids/—Treasury's Page for Kids, from the Treasury Department

History

www.si.edu/resource/tours/kidsguide—A Kid's Guide to the Smithsonian, from the Smithsonian Institution

www.cr.nps.gov/toolsfor.htm—Tools for Teaching, at Links to the Past, from the National Parks Service

Military

www.af.mil/aflinkjr/jr.htm—Air Force Kids Online, from the U.S. Air Force

www.lrp.usace.army.mil/kids/kids.htm—Just for Kids, from the U.S. Army Corps of Engineers, Pittsburgh District

Safety

www.usfa.fema.gov/kids/index.htm—USFA Kids Home Page, from the U.S. Fire Administration

Science and Technology

www.fetc.doe.gov/coolscience/index.htm—Cool Science, from the Federal Energy Technology Center

www.nsf.gov/od/1pa/nstw/kids/start.htm—Just for Kids, from the National Science Foundation

http://endangered.fws.gov/kids/index.html—Kid's Corner, from the U.S. Fish & Wildlife Service, Endangered Species Division

http://kids.msfc.nasa.gov/—Kids Space, from Liftoff To Space Exploration

www.nasa.gov/kids.html—NASA for Kids, from the National Aeronautics and Space Administration

Consider This

Banner Ads!

When you are on a Web site, it is very common to see rectangular ads for other Web sites or companies. These ads are often trying to sell you things. Scroll down and look for the information that is part of the Web site you've selected. If you accidentally go off the site because you clicked on a banner ad, then press Back and you'll return to the page you were on. Back is always a great way to go back to where you were. Ads on sites for kids are supposed to be clearly marked as such.

CHAPTER 5

Making Your Own Web Page

www.fastlaughs

What is an astronaut's favorite part of the keyboard?

Answer: The SPACE bar!

It's not really all that hard to make a simple Web page. There are two essentials to making your own Web page. First, you need somewhere to put your Web page (a host) so that friends and family can view your site. Second, you need the tools to create your page. Luckily, many online servers (including Netscape, Yahoo, and AOL) will provide everything you need to get your Web page online.

In most cases, you'll have to register with these servers (it's free) before you can start creating your home page. But after filling out a simple form (check with your parents before doing so!), you'll have access to the tools that will help you get your page up in a matter of minutes.

Popular places to go for Web site building are *www.angelfire.com*, *www.geocities.com*, and *www.bluelight.com*. Some kids' sites, such as *www.eplay.com* (check out the section called My Page), also have places to make a Web page. You can also go to *www.cnet.com*, which has a place called Web Building (click on Web Building in the yellow box at the bottom of the page). This site might be a little hard to understand. Check it out with your parents to learn more about making a Web site.

Another option is to use Web page authoring software, such as Microsoft's FrontPage or Filemaker's Home Page (Mac). These programs let you pick layouts and style elements from a host of templates. However, you will still need to find a host or location for your Web page. Check with your local Internet

Icon Groupie

An icon is a tiny drawing - a shorthand way to show a word instead of writing it out. Guess the computer term that each icon represents and fit the words into the grid. HELP: We left you several C-L-U-E-S.

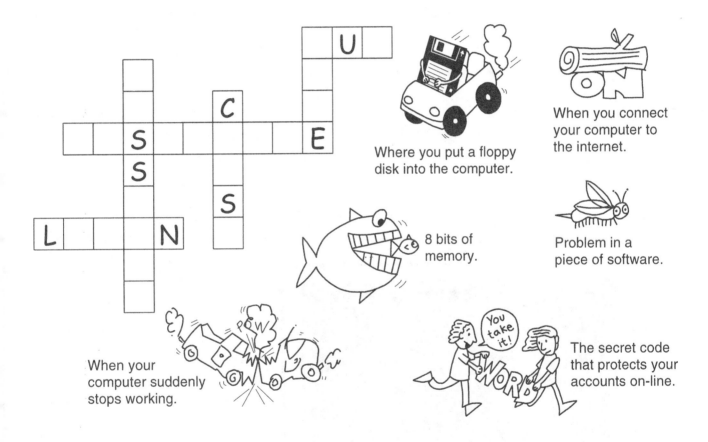

Where you put a floppy disk into the computer.

When you connect your computer to the internet.

8 bits of memory.

Problem in a piece of software.

When your computer suddenly stops working.

The secret code that protects your accounts on-line.

service provider; they might offer a certain amount of space (usually 5–10MB) for free.

Planning Your Web Site

Forget the computer stuff for now. Before you start learning the program to create your own site and checking out which online servers to go to, you need to plan your Web site.

Sit down with a pen and paper and go to it. It's not homework, because no one says you must have a Web site. So, have some fun!

The first thing to consider is why you want a Web site. What is its purpose? Do you want to teach people about something that you like? Do you want to share your hobbies with everyone? Do you want to tell jokes or riddles? Do you want to talk about your vacations and show people some neat photos of your trips? Perhaps you want to tell other kids which books, TV shows, movies, or even Web sites to check out. Whatever your reason, keep it in mind while you design the site and when you update it. If people don't know what the site is about, they may not keep reading.

Next, you should organize or arrange the Web site so it is easy to understand. You know how hard it is to find what you are looking for when your bedroom is a mess, so think of a Web site as a clean

You can swim all day in the sea of knowledge and still come out dry. Most people do.

-Norman Juster

room (and you don't even have to get off the chair to clean it). If the site is neat and the photos, quizzes, and everything else are easy to find, people will like the site. One idea is to put all of your photos on the right side and all of your text (words) on the left. Or perhaps you can have a list of computer games on the main page and then have your review of each game come up when visitors click on the name of a game. Hey, that rhymes! Perhaps you can have poems, stories, recipes. There are so many possibilities.

WORDS to KNOW

bells and whistles: special effects and fancy features on a Web site or a computer program.

You also need to explain things in clear short sentences. "Here is a quiz about the Backstreet Boys" or "This is the hotel where I stayed with my parents when we went to Walt Disney World." You can use icons (little pictures) for people to click on to find what they are looking for. You can also use a text menu, which is a list of places people can click on to find other things.

Building your Web site is like building a house, and the links are like doorways to other rooms. Plan what you will have in each link. Remember, don't overdo it. Too many links can confuse people. It also takes longer to get your Web site started. Build the first floor to the house before trying to build the second floor, the patio, and the attic.

If you make links to other pages, you can also decide which of those pages will link to each other. Just like some kitchens have two entrances, you can have more than one way to link to an area.

It's nice to use color, designs, moving headlines, and other fun computer designs (called **bells and whistles** by computer folks). Once again, remember, don't overdo it. Have you ever looked at a site that had so many things moving around, flashing, and blinking that you couldn't find what you were looking for?

A "bit" is the smallest unit of computer information there is. A bit is always either a one or a zero. If you put a bunch of bits together, it's called a "byte." How many bits make a byte? Use the decoder, below, to figure out the answer. HELP: The slash mark (/) in the message is the space between letters. A double slash mark (//) is the space between words.

Decoder:

A = 001   N = 0101
B = 011   R = 0
E = 1   S = 110
G = 010   T = 10
H = 01   Y = 1010
I = 100

10/01/1/0/1//001/0/1//

_____

1/100/010/01/10//

_____

011/100/10/110//

_____

100/0101//001//

_____

011/1010/10/1//

_____

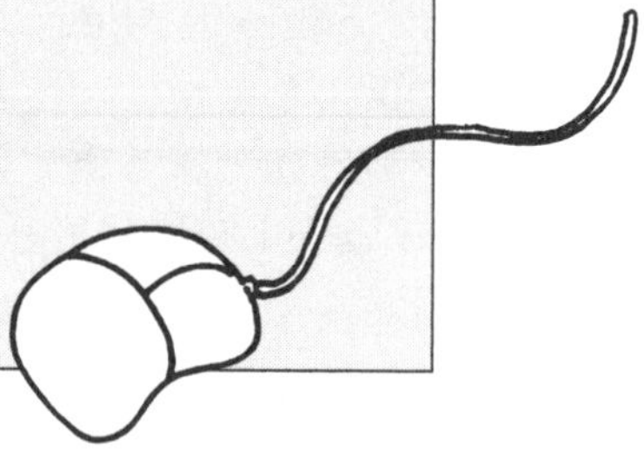

Look at other Web sites and write down what you like about them. Of course, you don't want to do the same thing, but you can get some ideas. Just as a house could have a bathroom that looks like the bathroom in your aunt's house, a kitchen that looks a little like your grandmother's, and a bedroom that is similar to your sister's room, your Web site can incorporate fun things from other sites.

WORDS to KNOW

HTML: stands for HyperText Markup Language, the language used to create Web sites.

Learning the Language

Now, here comes some tough stuff. Read it slowly and then write it down. This is very basic stuff to learn about **HTML**, which stands for HyperText Markup Language. If you don't understand it, that's okay. If you don't want to learn HTML, that's okay, too—we won't be upset. To be honest, we don't understand it all that well either!

The program for creating your own Web site is called HTML. It is a language that trans- lates to a Web page. You will need an Internet connection, a Web browser program like Microsoft Internet Explorer or Netscape Navigator, and a text program (a place to do your writing) like Microsoft Word or WordPerfect.

HTML is not that hard. It means that you have to put commands at the beginning and at the end of each thing you write. The commands are enclosed in angle

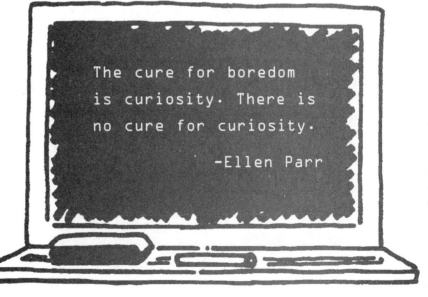

The cure for boredom is curiosity. There is no cure for curiosity.

-Ellen Parr

Web Words

How long will it take to download the information from your brain into the numbered puzzle grid? We left a few P-O-I-N-T-S and C-L-I-C-K-S to help you get around. HELP: All the answers are somewhere in this book!

ACROSS

1 Dads and _____ like to use the internet with their children
5 Shortcut way of typing "By the way…"
7 Finding your way from one site to another on the internet
8 An educational Web site has an address that ends in ". _____"
10 A large network of information, coming by computer, from all over the world
13 Shortcut way to write "HyperText Markup Language" (the language that describes a web page)
14 Software that your computer uses to look at web sites is called a "web _____"
16 Going around the internet looking at many different web sites is called "_____"
18 Your "Internet _____ Provider" is a company, like AOL, that hooks your computer up to the internet
21 Your "_____word" is a secret word used to pick up e-mail and get into on-line accounts
24 Some parents will set _____ limits so kids won't use the computer for hours and hours and hours
25 The internet allows two-way conversation. It is "_____."
28 The tool that lets your computer use the phone line to get on the internet
29 Shortcut way to write "Universal Resource Locator" (otherwise known as a web site address)
30 A commercial Web site has an address that ends in ". _____"
31 There are certain rules you must follow to stay _____ while using the internet
32 A connection from one web site to another. When you click on a "_____," you automatically travel to the other site.

DOWN

2 "_____" mail is a nick-name for paper letters sent through the post office
3 Parents can use a tool called "Net _____" to filter out unwanted or dangerous information before it gets to your computer
4 A Web site created by the government has an address that ends in ". ___"
6 WWW stands for "World _____ _____" (answer is 2 words)
9 Your computer hooks up to the internet over the _____ lines
11 A "search _____" helps you to look up information or find a web site. It's like a computer librarian!
12 "www.___cow" is a site for anyone who loves cows!
15 A place on the internet that someone creates to provide information
16 "www.simon_____.com" is the web site of book publishers Simon and Schuster
17 Never ever _____ out your name, address, or password on the internet
19 A place on the internet where you can have a conversation with other computer users
20 When you go to a web site, this is the first page you will see. It tells you what information the site has.
22 A little picture you can type on the computer using letters and punctuation marks
23 A list of choices
26 A computer program designed to make a computer "sick"
27 A letter that you send to someone over the internet

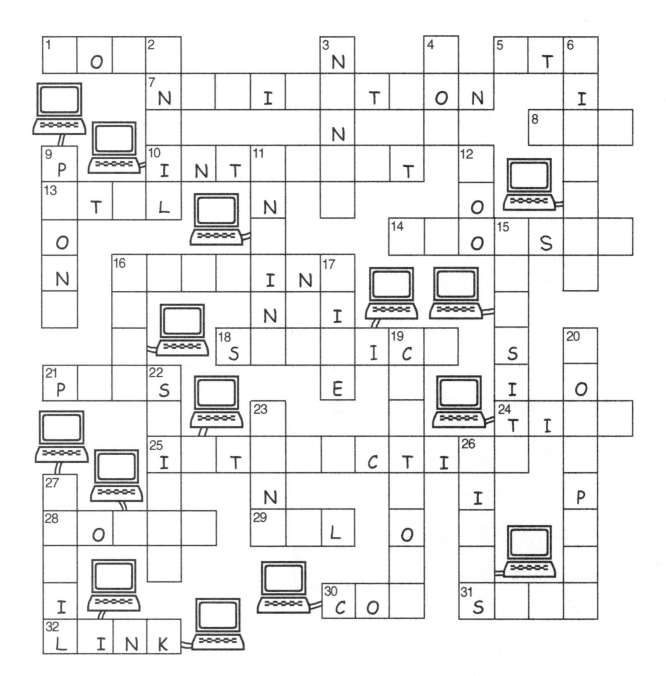

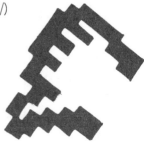

brackets (< >). You also put a slash (/) in front of the closing command within the brackets. For instance, you would put <HTML> to start the page reading to a special HTML program for Web sites. Then you type <TITLE> before your title and </TITLE> after your title to show where the title begins and ends.

Next, you put the main information, or "body," on your site. This is what you really want to say. So you type <BODY> and then type in all your stuff. Then put </BODY> when you want that part of the Web site to end. If that's all you want on the site, you type in </HTML>. There are also ways to put up links, photos, and other cool stuff. It's kind of like putting everything between bookends—one at one side and one at the other.

HTML takes some practice, just like learning to play a tough computer game. You can read books about HTML (*Make Your Own Web Page* by Ted Pedersen) or go to Web sites like *www.killersites.com* or *www.cwru.edu/help/introHTML/ toc.html*. Remember, you don't need to learn HTML to build a Web page if you go to the two sites just listed. But if you want to know the basics of building a site, HTML is not that hard to learn.

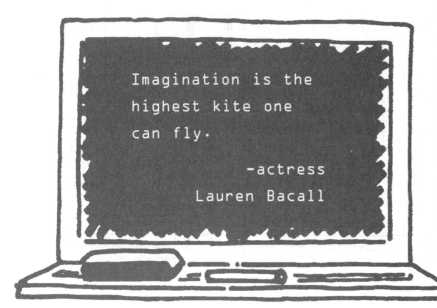

Imagination is the highest kite one can fly.

-actress
Lauren Bacall

Sample HTML Page

```
<HTML>
<TITLE> Your Own Web Page </TITLE>
<BODY> This is my own Web page. Isn't it cool? I'm writing
```
it in HTML. What do you think? I'm going to talk about hobbies,
games, and other neat stuff on my page. But for now, this is
just a way to show you how the commands look. When it
comes up as a Web page, all the commands (the stuff in
brackets) won't be there.
```
</BODY>
</HTML>
```
You can add **boldface** to your site with `<B>`.

You can also add a link, known as a hyperlink, by putting in
an anchor link. This is how you would link your page to your
best friend Fred's page:
```
<A HREF = "FREDSPAGE.HTML">
```
You also have to add a word that links the sites together
and gives the visitor something to click on. For example, you
could add the word *friendship*. Now, the link must end
with the same anchor tag it started with. (HREF stands
for hyperlinks reference, and the A is the anchor tag.)
So the whole thing would look like this:
```
<A HREF = "FREDSPAGE.HTML">FRIEND-
SHIP</A>
```

You can do a lot more, so HTML may be worth
checking out when you are ready.

Getting Started

Here are a few pointers to keep in mind once you get started:

1. Write in short, easy-to-understand sentences and paragraphs. When people read information on the Web, they don't like when it goes on and on and on and on . . . you get the point.
2. Pictures are nice, but don't overdo it. The more pictures you put on a Web site, the slower it will come up on other people's computers. You don't want visitors to get bored waiting for your Web page to appear. They might hit the Back button.
3. Don't give away identifying information. Don't put in your address, phone number, or personal information. In fact, clear the site with Mom and Dad first, just to make sure you haven't accidentally given away where you live or who you are (or any information about other family members). Use your first name only or make up a name. Chances are Jeeves, in the popular Ask Jeeves site, is not using his real name.
4. Look at the other sites and decide which ones you like and why. Keep in mind that some Web sites are very complicated and have been designed by professionals. Graphic artists and other people have spent countless hours working on them, so don't be disappointed if your first site doesn't measure up to Disney.com. They've invested millions of dollars in putting their sites together.
5. Manage your site. That means keep it up-to-date. You don't have to change it every day, but visitors will get bored if they look at your Web site every week or two and nothing ever changes. It's like designing a room other people to see. You always want it to look interesting so they'll come back.

Testing Your Site

Make sure your site works. Have some friends tell you if they can get it to come up on their computers. Also, ask them what they think of the Web site. Do they like it? Why? What do they think you should add or take away? If they tell you the things they don't like, don't get upset. The best way to improve your site is to get your visitors' honest opinions.

A Web site is great fun, but you need to be responsible, which means you need to remember a few things:

1. Don't give out personal information (other than your e-mail address if your parents say it's okay)
2. Don't say things that you wouldn't say in school or in public, including bad words or mean things about other people.
3. Keep updating the site.
4. Have fun!

Plan your web page. Take several sheets of paper and pretend they are your computer screen. Then map out what you want to go where on each page. Use a pencil with an eraser so you can change your mind. Web page designers change their minds again and again before the page has everything in the right place. You don't have to draw anything, just make a box and say "photo of my cat here" or "news of the day goes here". You might want to have a simple home page with a few places to click or you might want to start by holding the paper horizontally and drawing three lines dividing the page into three columns. Then you can put what you want in each column.

Use other sheets of paper to design the pages that you will click to from your homepage. Remember, too many photos makes the page slow and more difficult for people to download. If you keep it relatively simple at first, you can always add more.

- **Fun Web Sites**
- **For Parents—IMPORTANT**
- **A Web-Comfortable Family and Too Much of a Good Thing!**

Fun Web Sites

4CHILDREN.COM *www.4children.com*
ACME CITY *www.acmecity.com*
ALLOWANCENET *www.allowancenet.com*
AMERICA ONLINE *www.aolgames.com*
AMERICAN GIRL DOLLS *www.americangirl.com*
AMERICAN LIBRARY ASSOCIATION
 www.ala.org/ICONN/kcfavorites.html
ASK DR. MATH *www.askdrmath.com*
ASK JEEVES FOR KIDS *www.ajkids.com*
BIG BREW *www.bigbrew.com*
BONUS.COM *www.bonus.com*
THE BRONX ZOO *www.bronxzoo.com*
THE BUTTERFLY WEB SITE *www.butterflywebsite.com*
CANDYSTAND *www.candystand.com*
CARTOON NETWORK *www.cartoonnetwork.com*
THE CASE.COM FOR KIDS *www.thecase.com/kids/*
CHEF BOYARDEE *www.chefboy.com*
CHILDREN'S BUTTERFLY SITE *www.mesc.usgs.gov*
THE CIA HOMEPAGE FOR KIDS *www.cia.gov/cia*
COLORING.COM *www.coloring.com*
CONJUROR.COM *www.conjuror.com/magictricks/*
COOLMATH *www.coolmath.com*
COOLTOONS *www.cooltoons.com*
CRAYOLA.COM *www.crayola.com*
CYBER ZOOMOBILE *www.primenet.com/~brendel/index.html*
DICTIONARY.COM *www.dictionary.com*
DISNEY *www.disney.com*
EPLAY *www.eplay.com*
FLEETKIDS *www.fleetkids.com*
FOX KIDS *www.foxkids.com*
FEEZONE *www.freezone.com*
FUNBRAIN *www.funbrain.com*
FUNOLOGY *www.funology.com*
FUNSCHOOL *www.funschool.com*
HAMSTERDANCE *www.hamsterdance.com*

HARPER CHILDRENS *www.harperchildrens.com*
HBO4KIDS *www.hbo4kids.com*
HEADBONE ZONE *www.headbonezone.com*
KELLOGG'S *www.kelloggs.com*
KIDSNEWS *www.kidnews.com*
KIDS CLICK! *http://sunsite.berkeley.edu/kidsclick!/*
KIDSCOM *www.kidscom.com*
KIDS DOMAIN *www.kidsdomain.com*
KIDSITES.COM *www.kidsites.com*
KIDSSPACE *www.kidsspace.com*
LYCOS KIDS ZONE *www.lycoszone.com*
MAJOR LEAGUE BASEBALL *www.majorleaguebaseball.com* or
     www.majorleaguebaseball.com/u/baseball/mlbcom/kids/
MAKING FRIENDS *www.makingfriends.com*
MAMAMEDIA *www.mamamedia.com*
MARY-KATE AND ASHLEY *www.marykateandashley.com*
MCDONALDS *wwwmcdonalds.com*
MOOCOW *www.moocow.com*
NATIONAL WILDLIFE FEDERATION *www.nwf.org*
NICK JR. *www.nickjr.com*
NICKELODEON *www.nick.com*
NINTENDO *www.nintendo.com*
NOT JUST FOR KIDS *www.night.net/kids*
PETCO *www.petco.com*
ROUTE 6–16 *www.cyberpatrol.com/616*
SEA WORLD/BUSCH GARDENS *www.seaworld.org*
SIKIDS *www.sikids.com*
SIMONSAYSKIDS *www.simonsays.com*
SNAPPLE *www.snapple.com*
SPACEDAY *www.spaceday.com*
THUMB.COM *www.thumb.com*
VOLCANO WORLD *www.volcano.und.nodak.edu/*
WARNER BROTHERS *www.kids.warnerbros.com*
WEEKLY READER *www.weeklyreader.com*
THE WHITE HOUSE FOR KIDS *www.whitehouse.gov*
YAHOOLIGANS *www.yahooligans.com*
ZOOGDISNEY *www.zoogdisney.com*

For Parents—IMPORTANT

You've told your children not to talk to strangers or to get in a car with someone they don't know. You are probably somewhat vigilant about what television shows they watch and which movies you'll allow them to see. Now, thanks to modern technology, you have a new means of communication to monitor—the Internet.

The positive aspects of the Internet certainly outweigh the negatives. A wealth of information on numerous subjects waits at your child's fingertips. You no longer need to buy encyclopedias or run to the library every time your child needs research for a school project. The Internet hasn't replaced books, but it makes finding information a lot easier. It also provides great entertainment for any age level. And, unlike television, the Internet is interactive. There are numerous avenues to explore and fun things to do. It's well worth your time to explore the Internet with your child in much the same way you spend time reading together.

On the Internet, nobody knows you're a dog.

-Peter Steiner

Be sure to have a good understanding of the Internet before you go online with your child. Seek out child-friendly places like those mentioned in this book and search for topics and Web sites that you think might interest your child. Unfortunately, familiarizing yourself with the Internet is the lesser portion of your responsibility as a parent. In fact, many children are learning the Internet in school. They may be way ahead of you by the time you hit the "power" button for your joint venture.

You need to know how to protect them online. As we said earlier, you teach your children not to talk to strangers. On the Internet there are many strangers hiding behind user names and Web addresses. This is not to say your son or daughter may not make great friendships online. It is not to suggest that you watch your child's every online move until they are 21. It is a matter of taking precautions and playing it safe. The Internet spans the world and it is interactive.

You've probably heard stories of children (usually teens) who arrange to meet someone they've met online with disastrous consequences. It doesn't happen very often, but the Internet is still uncontrolled. You need to find ways to control it by finding appropriate software, and by guiding, educating, and monitoring your child.

A lot of people are making money on the Internet through many types of business ventures. Most are legitimate businesses; and many are from familiar companies. However, the pornography industry is also running rampant on the Internet. The number of pornography sites is staggering. They are not as well marked as the "adult video section" of the neighborhood video store. Accidentally typing in the wrong address can send your child to a site that is inappropriate. There are also Web sites that preach hate, racism, violence, and even have instructions on building and using weaponry. In essence, the Web covers the good and the bad. That is why you need to be in control.

Until you feel comfortable that your children are responsible enough to handle this type of wide-reaching medium on their own, you need to be there to teach them what

Consider This

A Community Effort

Talk with other parents. Share ideas about keeping the Internet safe for your kids. The task will be easier if everyone in your community establishes good rules for online behavior.

to do and what not to do. The Internet cannot serve as a babysitter. Unlike Nickelodeon, the program can change with the click of a mouse.

One of the most basic elements of the Web is navigation. While you're exploring the Internet together, teach your child a few key ways to get to where they want to go. The Favorite Places area might be an ideal corner of the computer world to stock with their special sites. As soon as you find a site they like, click on "Favorites," and add it to the list. Younger children are often quite happy to stick with what's familiar. They're not yet interested in, or aware of, the potential to explore. And with Favorite Places filled with sites like Disney.com and Nick.com, they'll have places to go and things to do.

Besides looking at interesting topics and playing games, you can help your children learn to use the Internet for researching their homework assignments as they get older. By the third or fourth grade, they'll find the Internet can help them discover lots of information about any subject. Be sure to monitor their searches or use a kids' search program. When you research a subject on the most popular search engines (like Excite or AOL), you'll find that you're overwhelmed by the number of responses you get.

The search engine goes through millions of documents or files and finds anything with a matching word. Many of the sites are inappropriate; others just don't have valid information. Some sites haven't been updated for years; others are simply trying to sell you things. You need to become familiar with the best places to look for homework help.

Consider This

Benefit of the Doubt

If your child stumbles onto something objectionable and asks you about it, it was probably an accident. Your best defense is to calmly explain why the site is not appropriate. Accidentally stumbling onto incorrect sites is not difficult. Adults do it quite often. Of course, you might get suspicious if it happens a lot.

Here are some kid-friendly search engines you can try:

- Kids Click! at *http://sunsite.berekley.edu/kidsclick!/*
- Route 6–16 at *www.cyberpatrol.com/616*
- Supersnooper at *www.supersnooper.com*
- Yahooligans at *www.yahooligans.com*

Once your kids are comfortable using these search engines, you'll be able to give them some independence. Drop by on occasion, because these sites are not always foolproof and they span a range of ages. Therefore, your child may be finding information that is too complicated. Sometimes you can specify age levels and sometimes you can't.

Consider This

Get a Second Phone Line!

It is hard for a family to survive with Internet service and only one telephone line. The benefits really outweigh the small expense to have a separate phone line put in for the Internet, regardless of whether children or adults are using it.

Get Some Protective Help!

You want to teach your child(ren) to use the Internet, but you can't sit with them constantly. And you are afraid to leave them alone, because you're worried that they'll stumble onto who knows what.

There are tools, in the form of programs, that can help. The following programs allow you to filter out unwanted material:

- Net Nanny at *www.netnanny,com*, (800) 340-7177
- Cyber Patrol at *www.cyberpatrol.com*, (617) 494-1200
- Cybersitter at *www.cybersitter.com*, (800) 388-2761

They are not foolproof. You still need to drop by now and then to see what is on the screen, but they do provide some peace of mind.

You can also go to a site called *www.getwisenet.org* and look at reviews of more than one hundred such tools. In fact, you can specify what you want to the tool to do by checking boxes such as Filters Sex, Filters Violence, and Limits Time.

The features of each software tool are listed, including whether they can be set up differently for different members of the family.

Chat Rooms

While it's very important to monitor your children as they become comfortable using the Web, it's also extremely important that you be nearby for the first chat room experience. Even though they may not want you cramping their style, you need to make sure that they are using monitored chat rooms for kids like those at Headbone Zone. In unmonitored chat rooms, they run the risk of encountering language that is highly inappropriate and engaging in conversations with adults posing as children.

Start off with basic ground rules. In fact, you might ask your children to sign a contract concerning chat room behavior. Remind them that this is important for their safety.

First, they must never give out any personal information. It is very dangerous to give out their name, phone number, address, school name or address, or post a picture or any other identifying information about themselves or any member of the family. This is important to remember for every aspect of the Internet—checking out chat rooms, surfing the Web, signing on message or bulletin boards, or registering for anything. When online they use their screen name, and that is it.

Consider This

At What Age?

Generally speaking, children under 10 or 11 should not be in chat rooms. That step will depend on how mature and responsible your child is.

How-To

Cybersnoop

Cybersnoop is a software program that allows you to look at a list of 2,000 sites that may be objectionable. Cybersnoop can tell you what sites your child has been going to, block sites you do not want them to have access to, and can even record chat. Depending on your child, you will be able to determine whether you need Cybersnoop and which functions you would use. To find out more, try *www.pearlsw.com*, or call (800) 732-7596.

Also, they must *never* give out their password. If they need to sign up to participate in a Web site or enter a contest, they should ask you to do so with them. Then you can determine that the site is valid and secure (meaning the information is not going farther than that Web site) and that the questions are not too personal.

Second, make sure your children know that they should *never* plan to meet someone in person whom they have met online. Only you, as a parent, can set up this type of meeting, once you've established that they are indeed dealing with another child.   Then you must be present at a first meeting in a public place. If you can e-mail the parents of the other child and at some point talk with them by phone, you will be able to alleviate some of your fears. Even adults are quite leery of meeting someone whom they have met on the Web. Relationships (and even marriages) have resulted from online meetings, but you must be very careful and always meet for the first time in a busy public place.

You'd be surprised at how easily information can be traced. One family was quite surprised when a cyber-police officer showed up at their door and said he found them because of what their daughter innocently posted in a chat room. She talked about a nearby monument, a large oak tree in her back-yard, her short four-block walk to school—and the cop figured out where she lived. Fortunately it was a cop, who warned the family to take precautions.

A Web-Comfortable Family and Too Much of a Good Thing!

Once you feel confident that your child can use the Web site alone, be a gadfly. Pop your head in once in a while

FUN FACT

History

Most browsers have a mysterious feature called History, which many users never bother with. It can tell you the last Web sites visited that day, previous days, and in some cases for weeks or months. If you've got a kid who seems to be in that "extra curious" stage, you might want to check out where he or she has been visiting online by hitting the History button.

whether he or she likes it or not. If you can talk about the Web and make it something that you share from the beginning, then your child might not mind your dropping by to see how things are going. Establish a bond. Tell your child about your experiences using the Internet for work or for communicating with a friend or relative. Then let him share Web-related stories. Keep the Internet a point of family discussion. Set the computer up in a family room instead of putting it in a child's bedroom—at least until he or she is a teenager. This keeps the experience family-oriented and open. It also keeps your child from overdoing it online.

Consider This

When the Internet Becomes a Real Problem

If your son or daughter is foregoing other activities, not keeping up with schoolwork, or shirking responsibilities, it may be time to pull the plug for a while. Also, if he or she is becoming overly involved with online relationships and friendships, be cautious.

One of the biggest concerns parents have today, especially with teenagers, is that their children are spending way too much time on the Internet. From day one, set time limits. The Internet is addicting at all ages, so curb the habit from the beginning. Like watching TV, the Internet should be part of their evening's activities, not all of it. You may even find yourself asking them, "Wouldn't you rather watch television for a while?" Not only do children and teens overuse the Internet, adults also spend hours sifting through pages of information, often at the expense of other activities.

E-Mail

Remind your kids that although it's great fun to send and receive e-mail, it can also be dangerous. E-mail from the wrong source can cause a computer virus that can wipe out your hard drive and destroy files that you are saving. You should look into anti-virus software like Norton Anti-Virus

Consider This

Mr. X

Remind your children and teens (and remember it yourself) that people on the Web may very likely not be who they claim they are. The same holds true for information—it may not be coming from a reputable source. Anyone can post information on the Web. That does not mean it is accurate.

(*www.symantec.com/nav/index.html*, (800) 441-7234), a software product that scans documents and programs on a regular basis and will detect all known viruses. McAfee Virus Scan (*www.network.com*, (800) 338-8754) is another popular software program that also detects viruses and provides updates.

Even with an anti-virus program, you must still teach your children never to open e-mail from anyone they do not know. Besides the lesser possibility of a new, unknown virus, there is the risk of questionable material. There are also Internet companies that want to "sign people up" and then send their information all over the net. Then you'll get lots of junk e-mail and SPAM (or online unwanted mass advertising) The same holds true for downloading anything from a source that is unfamiliar to you.

Lists can also be a big problem. Although an online mailing list may be from a company, it is usually set up as a "friendly" list between a number of people. Often these lists are put together to send jokes or even chain letters. The problem is that other people can get themselves added on to the list. As a result, lists grow to a point where most of the names are no longer familiar. Therefore, what was once friendly chat can turn into off-color jokes, sexual material, flames (people insulting each other online), or other unwanted information. It is often hard to get your name off a list, so don't be surprised if your child, despite his or her best efforts (and your best efforts), stays on the list. At that point, your child must learn how to delete e-mail without

opening it, which usually means clicking once to highlight the e-mail and hitting delete. You can always change your screen name as a last resort. However, this may mean rejoining some of the legitimate sites you like.

You should also explain that saving too much e-mail takes up space in the computer and will affect its operation. Asking your child to delete e-mail once he or she has finished reading it will avoid the problem.

On the positive side, kids can keep in touch with relatives more easily (and more inexpensively) than by telephone by dropping them a quick e-mail. Make this a shared activity with younger children. E-mailing people overseas is a particularly nice way to keep in touch at a very low cost.

Teach young children how to use e-mail and how to get into the habit of writing brief letters. Chances are, they'll be so anxious to send their e-mail that they won't want to say much anyway. Believe it or not, e-mail can help hone communications and even writing skills.

Quick Click

If every time you stroll by, your child quickly clicks the mouse and you see a main menu or a home page, he or she might be hiding something. Remember that you can always check out the last few sites visited. Most browsers have a History button that allows you to scroll back through several previous Web addresses.

Internet Tips for Parents

1. Set up the computer in a family room, rather than in a child's bedroom.
2. Do a little preliminary scouting and learning. It's better if you make the mistakes and find the wrong sites. Become comfortable and familiar with the Web before you begin teaching your child. Check out a few sites and look for age-appropriate places where your child might go.
3. Get off to a good start. Make the Internet a shared activity until your child is ready to go solo. Surf together, check out chat rooms together. You can play games, help with home-work, and even send e-mail to relatives and friends.
4. Remind your child to sit back from the screen some 15 to 18 inches in a position that won't leave him with an aching back.
5. Set time limits. Encourage your child to be active in other aspects of life, like playing outdoors, getting together with her friends, and so on.

There is no reason anyone would want a computer in their home.

-Ken Olson, DEC President, at the Convention of the World Future Society, 1977.

6. Monitor what's going on online. Once your child is flying solo, you can still drop by periodically and see what she is looking at. Most search engines also allow you to scroll back and look at the last several sites visited.
7. Be aware of the software your child is downloading for games or anything else. Remind her that it's possible to get a computer virus from unfamiliar downloads.

8. Try to limit your child's accessibility to e-commerce sites, which try to sell everything under the sun. Since most 9- or 10-year-olds aren't armed with credit cards (or shouldn't be), they should not have purchasing power. However, check your credit card statement closely. You'd be surprised at what some kids have ordered with their parents' credit card number.

   Some sites enable you to set up an account to give your child some buying power. Rocketcash *www.rocketcash.com* or Icanbuy *www.icanbuy.com* are two examples. These sites can help teach your child the value of money, how to spend it wisely, and even how to save it. You can monitor and cancel transactions. This is a good way to teach e-commerce (which is growing by leaps and bounds), if you feel your child is responsible enough to handle it.

9. Make sure your child knows that if he has a question or problem, you will help. Encourage him to tell you if he runs across objectionable material.

10. Don't preach. The Internet isn't something bad. It's a valuable aid that simply needs to be understood. *Preaching doesn't work anyway.*

www.fastlaughs

Why *did the computer stay home from school?*

Answer: It caught a virus!

Glossary

Banner ad: Advertisements for products and services in a bar near the top of a Web site or list of sites. Banner ads are usually in full color and sometimes flash to catch your attention.

Bells and whistles: Special effects and fancy features on a Web site or a computer program.

Chat room: Online places where a group of people can chat with each other in "real time" (that is, you are all on your computers at the same time). Usually chat rooms are set up to talk about a particular interest or hobby.

Cyberspace: The name for all of the online stuff going on "out there."

Download: To store a computer program from a Web site or disk to your computer hard drive.

E-mail: Letters you send and receive online.

Fan sites: Web sites about celebrities created for their fans.

FAQ: Short for "frequently asked questions." You will often see a FAQ list or link in programs or Web sites.

Favorites: A list of your favorite Web sites that you can access easily.

File: Where you store information on a computer.

Inbox: The place on your computer where your incoming mail arrives.

Interactive: You are an active participant and can make things happen or not happen. You don't just sit and watch the computer screen like you do watching TV.

Internet service provider: A company that hooks you up to the internet.

HTML: Stands for HyperText Markup Language, the language used to create Web sites.

Link (and hyperlink): They take you to other parts of a Web site or to other Web sites.

Mouse: The little gadget attached to your computer with a tail-like cord that moves the arrow around on your computer screen.

Navigate: Moving around the Internet.

Network: A group of computers that are linked together.

Newbie: Someone new to the chat room.

Point and click: The nickname for when you point your mouse arrow and click it to make something happen.

Reboot: To start your computer again.

Screen name: The fake name you create to remain anonymous when you chat online.

Scroll: Computer text rolling along the screen.

Search engine: A service that allows you to look things up on the Internet.

Secure site: A site that has a special program that allows you to send information or buy things without anyone else being able to see the information you provide.

Surfing: Looking around on the Internet.

Typos: Mistakes made in typing. These can be common in e-mail since you are usually writing quickly and it is considered informal. There are spell-check programs that will help you minimize typos, but they are considered no big deal in email.

URL: Stand for Uniform Resource Locator. It is the address for a Web site.

User friendly: What a software program or Web site is called when it's easy to find what you are looking for and to understand directions.

Virus: A program designed to mess up computers. Other programs, called "anti-virus software," have been created to recognize and destroy viruses.

Puzzle Answers

page 5 • **www.hiddennumbers**

Dear Grams,

Yesterday I went to a carnival at the zoo with my friends Leon and Ty(one). There was lots to do! We gazed into a mirrored ma(ze) r(o)om. (We didn't go in.) We watched (one) zebra and two bis(on) e(a)t a pile of hay with h(one)y. (Ty(one) thought the bison was ph(one)y.) They took meat from the free(zer) o(u)t to the li(one)ss. The li(on) e(v)en ate bacon! We played Spin The Wheel and Leon won a pr(ize) r(o)se. (It made him sneeze.) It was so hazy and hot we wanted to buy a dozen ice cream c(one)s from a man with a free(zer) o(n) wheels. (We didn't.) So(on) every(one) but me was tired. They decided to doze(on e)mpty benches, but I rode (on e)very ride. I went on the "Crazy Da(ze) Ro(deo)" machine twice!

Love, Andrew

P.S. At night, every sign was ne(on) except for (one)!

page 9 • **Point and Click**

page 11 • **Follow That Link**

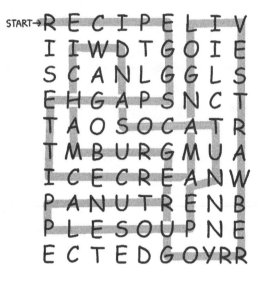

page 15 • **www.correctaddress**

Puzzle Answers

page 26 • **Keyboard Code**

1. J W K 4
   N A M E

2. W R R 5 4 E E
   A D D R E S S

3. E F U 0 0 P
   S C H O O L

4. - U 0 J 4   J 8 K H 4 5
   P H O N E   N U M B E R

5. - W E E 3 0 5 R
   P A S S W O R D

6. - U 0 6 0
   P H O T O

page 21 • **Interesting!**

The internet is INTERACTIVE. It allows two-way communication!

1. The class after "beginning", but before "advanced"' .... INTERMEDIATE

2. A radio system that lets people talk between different rooms in a house .... INTERCOM

3. To break into a conversation and change the subject .... INTERRUPT

4. A rest period between the first and second half of a concert. .... INTERMISSION

5. A meeting where one person asks the other person questions about themselves .... INTERVIEW

6. To stop something on its way from one place to another....................... INTERCEPT

Puzzle Answers

page 24 • www.slowpoke

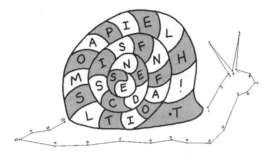

$\underline{THE}$ $\underline{POST}$ $\underline{OFFICE}$

$\underline{SENDS}$ $\underline{SNAIL}$ $\underline{MAIL}$ $\underline{!}$

page 34 • www.delete-it

~~Deer~~ Hello Marta,

I can't ~~just~~ wait to see ~~around~~ you at camp ~~the~~ next week ~~bend~~. ~~Won't~~ remember to bring ~~up~~ pictures of your ~~same~~ new baby ~~sitter~~ brother.

Your best ~~curl~~ friend,

Teresa :-)

page 39 • The World at Your Fingertips

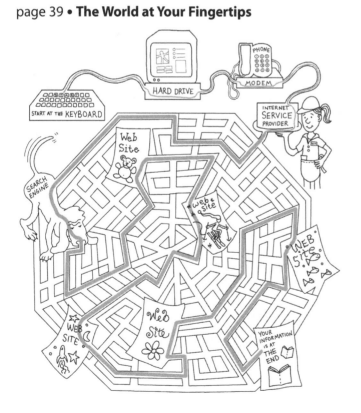

page 46 • Good Site, Bad Site

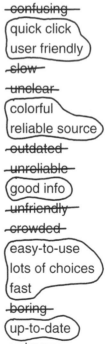

~~confusing~~
quick click
user friendly
~~slow~~
~~unclear~~
colorful
reliable source
~~outdated~~
~~unreliable~~
good info
~~unfriendly~~
~~crowded~~
easy-to-use
lots of choices
fast
~~boring~~
up-to-date
~~unknown~~

Puzzle Answers

page 48 • **www.smiley**

B-) — person winking
8:-) — girl with hairbow
:-)> — man with bowtie
8) — Uncle Sam
:8) — kid with braces
=I:-) — pig
:-# — man with beard
>:-) — frog
:-)8 — person with glasses
;-) — alien

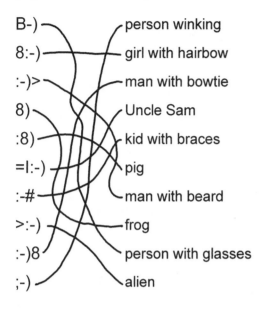

page 43 • **www.screename**

screen name:	profile:
laffalot	likes comic books
cr8tv	artistic
shutterbug	takes photos
surfkid	goes on-line a lot
123go	runs races
pbj	makes own lunch
ribbit	has pet frog
ticktock	likes clocks
topfloor	lives in apartment
hissssss	has pet snake
dribbler	plays basketball

page 59 • **Same Site?**

page 72 • **www.sillysite**

address in code:
xxx.gjtizebodf.dpn

real address:
www.fishydance.com

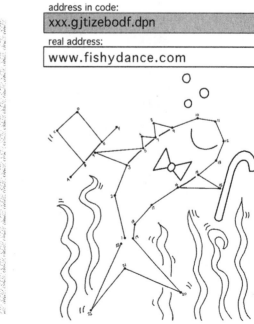

129

Puzzle Answers

page 62 • **www.computergraphics**

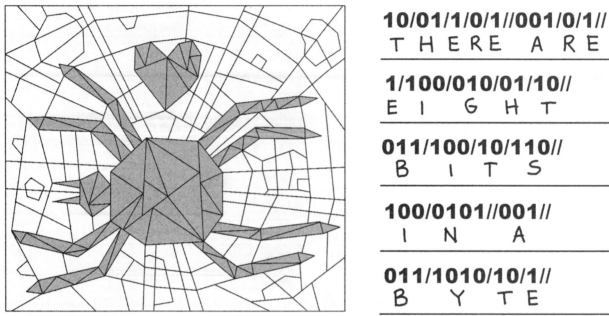

page 98 • **www.itsyBITsy**

10/01/1/0/1//001/0/1//
T H E R E   A R E

1/100/010/01/10//
E I   G H T

011/100/10/110//
B   I   T   S

100/0101//001//
I   N   A

011/1010/10/1//
B   Y   T E

page 95 • **Icon Groupie**

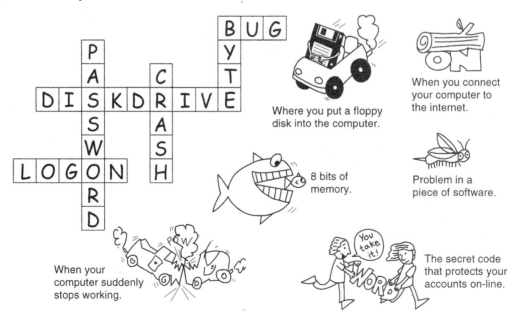

Where you put a floppy disk into the computer.

When you connect your computer to the internet.

8 bits of memory.

Problem in a piece of software.

When your computer suddenly stops working.

The secret code that protects your accounts on-line.

Puzzle Answers

page 100-101 • **Web Words**

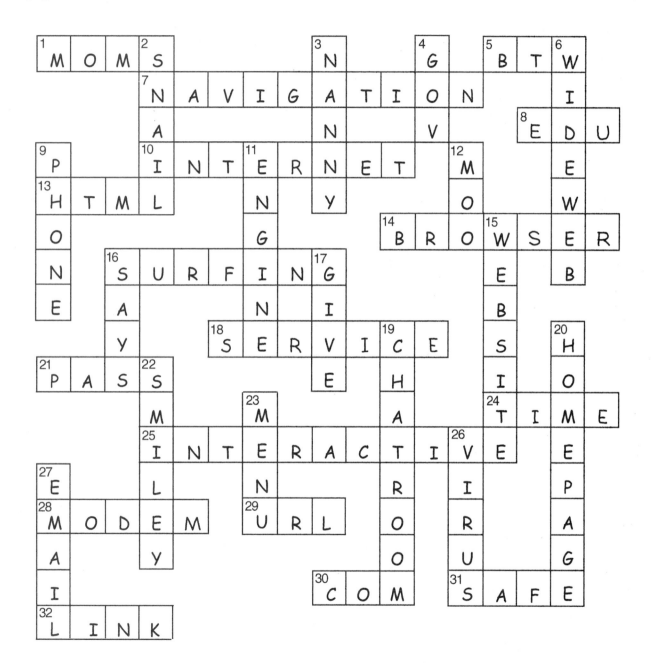

A

abbreviation, e-mail, 32–33
Acme City, 56
activities
   Interesting!, 21
   offline/online activity book, 23
   www.moviereview, 71
   www.screename, 43
   www.smiley, 48
addresses, Web, 6–9
Air Force Kids Online, 91
Allowancenet, 56–57
America Online, 57
American Girl Dolls, 57
American Library
   Association, 58
anti-virus software, 117–18
Ask Dr. Math, 58
Ask Jeeves for Kids, 58, 60

B

banner ads, 38, 91
bits, 98
Bog Brew, 60
Bonus.com, 60–61
bookmarks (Favorites), 6, 7,
   112
Bronx Zoo, 61
Butterfly Web Site, 63

C

call waiting, 35
Candystand, 63
Cartoon Network, 63–64
Case.com for Kids, 64
Charlie's Corner, 90
chat rooms, 27, 29–30, 32
   etiquette, 30, 32

monitoring of, 29
rules for, 30
safety in, 114, 116
screen names in, 29
Chef Boyardee, 64
Children's Butterfly Site,
   64–65
CIA Homepage for Kids, 65
Coloring.com, 65
computer viruses, 26, 117–18
Conjuror.com, 66
Cool Science, 91
Coolmath, 66
Cooltoons, 66–67
Crayola.com, 67
Cyber Zoomobile, 67
Cybersnoop, 115
cyberspace, 3

D

Dictionary.com, 67–68
Disney, 68–69
domain names, 8, 20
downloads, 10, 12

E

e-mail, 20–35
   abbreviations, 32–33
   capital letters in, 26
   chat rooms, 27, 29–30, 32
   club, 16
   and computer viruses, 26,
     117–18
   mailboxes, 33
   receiving, 25–27
   replying to, 25, 31
   safety, 117–19
   sending, 22–23, 25

tips, 23
workings of, 20, 22
Eplay, 69
etiquette, chat room, 30, 32

F

fan sites, 42, 44
FAQs, 32
Favorites, 6, 7, 112
FBI Kids' and Youth
   Educational Page, 90
files, 12
filtering software, 113–14, 115
Fleetkids, 69
Follow that Link (puzzle), 11
4children.com, 56
Fox Kids, 70
Freezone, 70
Funbrain, 73
Funology, 73
Funschool, 73

G

games, online, 51
Good Site, Bad Site
   (puzzle), 46
government Web sites, 90–91

H

Hamsterdance, 73–74
Harper Childrens, 74
HBO4kids, 74
Headbone zone, 74–75
home page, 8
HTML (HyperText Markup
   Language), 4, 99, 102–3
   sample page, 103
hyperlinks, 10

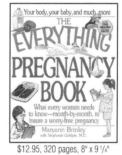

EVERYTHING®

The Everything® Kids' Money Book
by Diane Mayr

From allowances to money gifts, from lemonade stands to lawn-mowing businesses, *The Everything® Kids' Money Book* tells kids how to make money, save money, and spend money. It also has fascinating information about currency, an introduction to the stock market, and even some fun money-based games. Basically, this book is filled with everything a kid would want to know about money.

Trade paperback, $9.95
1-58062-322-0, 144 pages

The Everything® Kids' Puzzle Book
by Jennifer A. Ericsson & Beth L. Blair

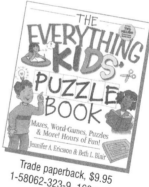

Stuck inside on a rainy day? Trapped in a car for a long trip? Just love puzzles? This is your book! From crosswords to mazes to picture puzzles, this book is filled with hours of puzzling fun. As an added bonus, every space that doesn't have a puzzle in it is filled with fascinating facts and funny jokes. You'll never be bored with *The Everything® Kids' Puzzle Book* by your side!

Trade paperback, $9.95
1-58062-323-9, 160 pages

See the entire Everything® series at www.adamsmedia.com/everything